The
Life and Struggles of
Negro Toilers

By
GEORGE PADMORE

Published by the R.I.L.U. Magazine for the
International Trade Union Committee of Negro
Workers   London, 1931

TONBRIDGE PRINTERS AND BOOKBINDERS
PEACH HALL WORKS   TONBRIDGE

CONTENTS

PART III

CHAPTER V

PART IV

CHAPTER VI

Revolutionary Perspectives

INTRODUCTION

IT has been estimated that there are about 250 million Negroes in the world. The vast majority of these people are workers and peasants. They are scattered throughout various geographical territories. The bulk of them, however, still live on the continent of Africa—the original home of the black race. There are, nevertheless, large populations of Negroes in the *New World*. For instance, there are about 15 millions in the United States, 10 millions in Brazil, 10 millions in the West Indies, and 5 to 7 millions in various Latin-American countries, such as Colombia, Honduras, Venezuela, Nicaragua, etc., etc.

The oppression of Negroes assumes two distinct forms : on the one hand they are oppressed as a class, and on the other as a nation. This national (race) oppression has its basis in the social-economic relation of the Negro under capitalism. National (race) oppression assumes its most pronounced forms in the *United States of America*, especially in the Black Belt of the Southern States, where lynching, peonage, Jim-Crowism, political disfranchisement and social ostracism is widespread ; and in the *Union of South Africa*, where the blacks, who form the majority of the entire population, have been robbed of their lands and are segregated on Reserves, enslaved in Compounds, and subjected to the vilest forms of anti-labour and racial laws (Poll, Hut, Pass taxes) and colour bar system in industry.

The general conditions under which Negroes live, either as a national (racial) group or as a class, form one of the most degrading spectacles of bourgeois civilisation.

Since the present crisis of world capitalism begun the economic, political and social status of the Negro toilers are becoming ever worse and worse. The reason for this is obvious : the imperialists, whether American, English, French, Belgian, etc., etc., are frantically trying to find a way out of their difficulties. In order to do so, they are not only intensifying the exploitation of the white workers in the various imperialist countries by launching an offensive through means of rationalisation, wage cuts, abolition of social insurance, unemployment, etc., but they are turning their attention more and more towards Africa and other black semi-colonies (Haiti, Liberia), which represent the last stronghold of world imperialism. In this way the bourgeoisie hope to unload the major burden of

5

the crisis on the shoulders of the black colonial and semi-colonial masses.

Furthermore, as the majority of the Negro workers in the United States and the colonies are still largely unorganised, thanks to the treachery and betrayal of the *American Federation of Labour* and the so-called progressive Mustie group in the United States, the social-fascist labour bureaucrats of the *Amsterdam International*, the *II International*, and the black reformist trade union leaders (Kadalie and Champion in South Africa, Randolph and Croswaith in the United States), as well as the national reformist misleader, Marcus Garvey, the Negro toilers are experiencing great difficulties to-day in withstanding the ruthless offensive of the international imperialists. Despite these handicaps the Negro masses, goaded into desperation by the inhuman conditions forced upon them on the one hand, and inspired by the revolutionary movement on the other, are beginning to wake up and assume the counter-offensive against their oppressors.

We can already see the beginnings of a conscious effort on the part of these Negro masses to consolidate their fighting forces, and to bring them into closer contact with the advanced ranks of the international revolutionary proletariat, by the holding of a conference in *Hamburg, Germany*, in July, 1930.

This was the first *International Conference of Negro Workers* which had ever been convened. At this conference Negro delegates from different parts of Africa, the United States, West Indies and Latin America not only discussed trade union questions, but dealt with the most vital problems affecting their social and political conditions, as for example the expropriation of land by the imperialist robbers in Africa ; the imposition of Head and Poll taxes ; the enslaving of toilers through Pass laws and other anti-labour and racial legislation in Africa ; lynching, peonage and segregation in the United States ; as well as unemployment, which has thrown millions of these black toilers on the streets, faced with the spectre of starvation and death.

In view of the present world situation, it is necessary to describe the *Life and Struggles of the Negro Toilers*, so that the workers in the metropolitan countries under whose imperialism these masses live will be better able to make themselves acquainted with some of the methods which the capitalists of the "mother" countries adopt to enslave the black colonial and semi-colonial peoples. For it is only by knowing these facts will the revolutionary working classes in Europe and America realise the danger ahead of them.

It is also necessary for the workers in the capitalist countries to understand that it is only through the exploiting of the colonial workers, from whose sweat and blood super-profits are extorted, that the imperialists are able to bribe the reformist and social-fascist trade union bureaucrats and thereby enable them to betray the struggles of the workers.

The purpose of this pamphlet is threefold :

(1) Briefly to set forth some of the conditions of life of the Negro workers and peasants in different parts of the world ; and

(2) To enumerate some of the struggles which they have attempted to wage in order to free themselves from the yoke of imperialism ; and

(3) To indicate in a general way the tasks of the proletariat in the advanced countries so that the millions of black toilers might be better prepared to carry on the struggles against their white imperialist oppressors and native (race) exploiters, and join forces with their white brothers against the common enemy—World Capitalism.

PART I

CHAPTER I

AFRICA

WITH the exception of Abyssinia and Liberia, the entire continent of Africa is completely under the domination of various imperialist Powers. GREAT BRITAIN, FRANCE, BELGIUM and PORTUGAL control the largest and most important sections of the continent. SPAIN and ITALY also have smaller colonies in Africa. The Northern territories of Africa—EGYPT, MOROCCO, TRIPOLI, ALGERIA, TUNIS, etc., etc., are inhabited by Arabic-speaking peoples, while the remaining sections of the continent are populated by various black tribes, generally referred to as Negro or Negroid.

Black Africa can therefore be divided into South, East, West and Central Africa, in contradistinction to the North, which is referred to as *Arab Africa*.

In this chapter we shall briefly describe some of the most glaring conditions and forms of oppression of Negro toilers under various imperialist governments in Black Africa.

I.—BRITISH SOUTH AFRICA

South Africa includes the Union of South Africa (which is a dominion of the British Empire), Basutoland, Bechuanaland, North and South Rhodesia, Swaziland and former German South-West Africa (a mandate under the Union Government), all of which cover an area about half the size of Europe. *The Union of South Africa* is the most important section in this part of the continent. It has an area of 471,917 square miles and is made up of four provinces : Cape Colony, Natal, Transvaal and Orange Free State. The population, according to the census of 1921, was estimated at 1,519,488 whites and 5,409,192 non-whites. Of these non-Europeans there are 4,697,813 Bantu natives, 165,731 Asiatics (mostly East Indians) and 545,548 people of mixed blood.

South Africa is a country of tremendous natural resources. Gold, diamonds, coal, tin and other valuable minerals are found in abundance. Its agricultural and pastoral products are also of great economic importance. This is why the country was stolen from the natives and plundered by the Europeans.

Politically the country is under the complete domination of English and Boer imperialists, who exploit the native population in the most brutal manner. In order to do this the South African bourgeoisie have imposed upon the native population what is known as the *Reserve* and *Compound* systems, together with a number of repressive anti-labour and racial laws.

1. *Land Robbery*

The *Reserve System* is the policy whereby all of the best lands have been taken away from the natives and turned over to white farmers. The natives are then gathered together on tracts of unfertile territory specially reserved for them. Because of the unproductive character of the land they are unable to produce enough food to feed themselves, and therefore they are forced to go and work for the European farmers and industrialists.

The European population of $1\frac{1}{4}$ million owns more than 80 per cent. of the land in the Union. The native population of $5\frac{1}{2}$ million owns less than 20 per cent., the reserves scheduled under the *Native Land Act* of 1913 being little more than $12\frac{1}{2}$ per cent. of the total.

The *Native Land Act* of 1913 had as its object to preserve the former status pending further legislation, with the promise that additional land for natives would be forthcoming. This promise has not yet been fulfilled. Purchase by natives, even in certain reserved areas, is allowed only by special permission of the Government. A special disability is that, owing to the restricted area in which purchase is even possible, prices are frequently raised against natives. Many owners willing to sell hold on until they get their price, knowing that natives cannot obtain land elsewhere.

In spite of statements to the contrary, figures show that existing native reserves are inadequate and overcrowded. The following figures represent the position at present :

The average density of population in the Union for all races was in 1926 14.64 per square mile.

The average density in typical native areas is as follows :

(*a*) *Transkei*—58.59 per square mile ; in one district, 102.91.

(*b*) *Natal and Zululand* (non-European)—36.63 ; in the *Inanda District*, 150.

(*c*) In the *Glen Grey District of the Cape*, which is surveyed and which contains 8000 allotments, there was in 1926 a waiting list of about 4000 landless natives. Some of these are now provided for, and are paying a quit-rent high enough to cover amortisation of a purchase price rendered notoriously high by farmers who were able to hold out for their own price.

(*d*) *Transvaal Native Areas*—70 to 90 per square mile.

(*e*) The *Orange Free State* provides 244.3 square miles for a native population of 440,000 in 1926, of whom far too many exist precariously in town locations, preferring these to the bad conditions for labour tenants prevailing on European farms.

On the borders of the Union, in *Swaziland*, two-thirds of the land is owned by European concessionaries, leaving 2,000 square miles for 120,000 natives, i.e., 60 per square mile (1926). The concessionaries provide a certain amount of employment, but wages are terribly low.

The many evictions and removals from European farms which followed the passing of the *Native Land Act*, 1913, led to further pressure on the Reserves ; and to a drift to town slums and urban location.

Conditions of tenure differ in various parts of the Union. There is extreme insecurity of tenure on all farms, which affects nearly two million natives, who can never gain secure homes, even for old age, after a lifetime service.

The life of the black farm labourers is hardly distinguishable from serfdom. In return for cultivating a piece of land allotted to the native by the white farmer the blacks are made to pay exorbitant rent or otherwise work without wages for the greater portion of the year for his white master. No matter how badly the landlord treats his serfs they are not permitted to leave the farm, for the *Masters and Servants Act*, which governs the relationship between employer and employee, makes it an offence for a black worker to break a " contract " entered into with a white employer.

We are informed of cases where the farmers, when they need labour, offer liberal terms of employment, but when the natives have engaged themselves the farmers turn round and say the law does not allow them to make such terms and absolutely refuse to give effect to the contract. This often leads to criminal action, with the result that natives are either imprisoned or evicted from the farms.

The tendency is for these laws to be stiffened in their action against the native. For instance :

(1) In 1926 the " squatter " was brought even more under " control " by being made a " servant."

(2) A new Bill designed by the Minister for Justice "proposes to add the possibility of lashes to fine or imprisonment as a punishment for breach of contract by a native."

Because of the congestion of the Reserves which adds to the famine condition always prevalent, thousands of blacks are forced to also migrate into industrial centres in order to find employment.

2. *Industrial Exploitation*

The following figures give an estimate of the number of black and white workers engaged in the basic industries in 1927 :

		Whites :	*Blacks :*
(1)	Gold	21,694	199,612
(2)	Diamond	14,638	60,918
(3)	Coal	1,744	44,079
(4)	Electric Power Co.	917,917	3,066

According to the Johannesburg Joint Council, " these urbanised industrial natives are governed by the *Masters and Servants Law* which, in the Transvaal, is fifty years old.

Under this law breach of contract of service is a criminal offence for the native worker, but not for the European employer.

Another law known as the *Colour Bar Act* (Mines and Works Act (1911), Amendment Act (1926)) gives power to close skilled occupation to natives. Its declared purpose is the segregation of natives in Reserves. (From 50 to 70 per cent. of the adult male population of the Reserves, and an increasing number of the women, are necessarily away from home at work for six or nine months per annum.) The general effect of the Act is to destroy all hope for the native to advance beyond menial labour, whatever his capacities may be, and to discourage the training of native labourers by employers.

Pass-bearing natives (i.e., the vast majority of the workers) are excluded from the working of the *Industrial Conciliation Act* of 1924. That is to say, no native industrial organisation has the legal recognition accorded to European Trades Unions, and so far as the native worker is concerned there can be no such thing as collective bargaining, whatever his grievances may be.

The average wage for European workers in the coal mining industry is between 20 shillings and 24 shillings *per day*, while that of the natives is 40 to 50 shillings *per month*. The same disproportion in wages exists in other basic industries. A European worker gets an average wage of about 295 pounds sterling per year, while a black worker receives 30 pounds. Wages among black and white factory workers also reflect the same disproportion. For example, in 1924 there were 66,189 white factory workers in South Africa who received an average of 246 pounds per year. During the same period 116,699 non-Europeans were employed in factories at the rate of 48 pounds per annum. Exclusive of the exploitation of the black workers in the form of low wages, long hours, etc., the conditions under which the Negro workers are forced to work, especially in the mining industries, are most demoralising and devitalising. In the gold and diamond regions of the Transvaal, thousands of natives are housed in military-like barracks known as *Compounds*. These *Compounds* are kept in the most filthy and insanitary condition, which, added to the bad food, mostly maize with salt, supplied the men, contribute largely to tuberculosis and other social and industrial diseases. A few years ago the conditions were so awful that the death rate was exceedingly high. The bourgeoisie became alarmed over this rapid depletion of their black slave labour, so they introduced certain " reforms " in the nature of medical inspection. However, as late as 1927 there were 44,347 births recorded among the Europeans in South Africa, and 16,627 deaths, while among the non-Europeans there were 51,077 births and 45,219 deaths. In some industrial areas the native infantile death rate is 750 per thousand. These vital statistics are living indications of the difference in the standards of living which exist between the two races. During the period that the Negro workers are employed in the mines they are not permitted to leave the Compounds, which are surrounded by barbed wire fences with armed guards at the gates. At the completion of their terms of service each worker is forced to swallow a dose of castor oil which would make even Mussolini shiver. This is done for the purpose of purging out any diamonds which the native might have concealed in his system!

In view of the present economic crisis in South Africa, which has greatly affected the industrial life of the country, a committee was recently appointed by the Native Affairs Dept. of the Government for the purpose of investigating the labour situation and to find a solution for the unemployment problem. The committee estimated the native labour force at 644,000, in addition to which there are about 275,000 Negroes imported into the country from surrounding territories. This labour was largely utilised in agriculture and the lighter industries in the urban areas. As a result there was a general shortage of labour in the mines. In the Western and South-Western part of Cape Province the labour supply was inadequate, due to the wholesale migration of natives, who were running away from the brutal rationalisation methods to which they are being subjected in the industries in this part of the country. In view of this the committee recommended that immediate steps be taken to prevent the natives from running away and to supply the demands of the mining companies, which require a labour force of about 300,000 native miners. There are only 190,000 such miners in the Witwatersrand mining district. For the purpose of complying with the demands of the mine-owners, the Government is taking active steps to force the natives to remain in the mining areas. This is being done by re-enacting various anti-labour laws and increasing taxation.

3. Political and Social Oppression

In order to obtain the money to pay the *Head and Poll* taxes, the blacks are forced to put up with the inhuman conditions imposed upon them in industry. Furthermore, whenever they attempt to run away they are immediately arrested by the police and turned over to their employers. This is done under a system known as the *Pass Law*, which makes it an offence for a black worker to walk the streets of any industrial city in South Africa unless he has a passport showing that he is in the service of some white capitalist. Through these czarist methods of police terrorism, millions of Negro toilers in South Africa are enslaved within their own country.

The following is a brief summary by Tymzo-shi, the Bantu

writer, on the twelve " badges " of slavery which the Negro toilers are compelled to carry about with them :

(1) *Identification Pass* (Natal)—This has to be carried by all natives in Natal for identification. It is a monthly document for which two shillings is paid per month.

(2) *Travelling Pass*—Carried by all male natives wishing to travel; in the case of rail a native has to produce this pass before a ticket is issued to him. Certain ticket issuers will demand also his poll-tax receipt. Thus the native is often embarrassed and does not know what form of " pass " is actually required before he may travel.

(3) *Six Days' Special Pass* (Permit to Seek Work)—When a native arrives in a town to look for work, or leaves service, he is given a six days' " special " to seek work. After the expiration of this period and failure to get a job his " special " is again endorsed for another six days. Should he again fail to obtain employment, he is " ordered " to another area by the police.

The authorities do not care how he gets there. All they care about is that he has to go there or suffer arrest or imprisonment. This is one of the cruellest of the pass laws.

(4) *Monthly Pass*—This is a contract of service to be carried by all native labourers, for which the employer has to pay two shillings a month. On this pass are inscribed the worker's name, father's name, tribe, chief, place of abode, poll tax—whether paid or not, and scale of wages—whether daily, weekly or monthly.

(5) *Daily Labourers' Pass*—This has to be held by all natives who carry on business. They pay two shillings per month, but the absurdity of the document is that while a native who carries on such private business of his own can issue " special passes " to other natives, he cannot supply himself with a " special pass " !

If he desires to go to another area, or to be out after 9 p.m., he has to apply to the Pass Office for his " special." Suppose this man is a painter, and is called on Saturday afternoon to do an urgent job, he cannot get away before the Pass Office opens on the following Monday. By then his job has taken wings ! Suppose his wife be so unfortunate as to give birth to a child after 9 p.m., he cannot leave his home to call the doctor or the nurse. If he does, he will be arrested and convicted, according to law.

(6) *Day Special Pass*—Every native who wishes to visit an area other than the one in which he resides has to carry a " special pass " stating how long he will be on such a visit.

(7) *Night Special Pass*—A native has to carry this if he wants

to be out after 9 p.m.   The employer can refuse to grant
this pass if he likes—as many do—and the woiker has either
to go at his own risk or to go to bed.

(8) *Trek Pass*—This applies almost entirely to farm labourers
when they leave one farm or district for another.

(9) *Location Visitors' Permit Pass*—A native who visits any
location has to get a permit from the Location Superintendent.   If this official is against revolutionary organisations he refuses the permit should the visitor be an
organiser or member of such bodies.

(10) *Lodgers' Permit*—Natives are allowed to become residents
of municipal locations only if they have paid from one
shilling and sixpence to two shillings and sixpence per
month " lodgers' permit " for themselves and families.
All natives over 18 years of age are subject to this tax.

(11) *Poll Tax Receipt Pass*—This is procurable on payment of
one pound per annum in urban areas and one pound ten
shillings in rural areas.   The receipt has to be produced
on nearly every occasion when the other passes must be
shown to the police or other agents of the imperialists.

(12) *Exemption Pass*—This is the " Big Boss " of all passes.
It is supposed to exempt the bearer from native law and
all other passes, but it does not. . . . Wherever the bearer
goes he will still be asked for his pass like the native who
has no such " exemption."

Added to these repressive measures there are special laws which
provide that every native must work 90 days every year free for
a European capitalist.

" Justice " in South Africa can only be compared to " justice "
in the Southern States of the U.S.A.   Negroes are not only
economically suppressed, but just because of this their political
and social status is negligible.   There is no law in South Africa
which a white man is bound to respect if it applies to the Negro.
If a white employer kills one of his Negro slaves all the court asks
of him is a fine.   But if the situation is the reverse then the Negro
is made to pay the " full penalty of the law " with his life.   Another
method by which Negroes are misused is before the police courts.
The magistrates make it a special point of duty to inflict severe
punishments upon the natives.   For example, just recently a South
African magistrate fined a poor native worker £7 10s., with the
alternative of six weeks' hard labour, simply because the man forgot
to carry one of the above described passes with him.   In sentencing
the Negro the magistrate said : " *You think you are too swanky
to carry passes.   All these rosettes and fountain pens of yours are
just to attract attention.   You dress yourselves as though you were
earning £20 a month and not £2 10s.   However, I never fail to make
men like you remember occasions such as this.*"

Politically, the status of the Negroes can be described as follows :

In the Cape, the franchise is based on the principle of racial equality. There is an educational test of a simple nature, and a voter must also have a property or wage-earning qualification. These tests do, in fact, exclude many native voters. The number of native voters is at present about 14,000 out of a total native population of 1,500,000, while of the coloured population (including Indians) of 435,000 nearly 27,000 are registered voters. In Natal, while the natives and coloured people may legally acquire the vote on certain conditions, in practice they are almost entirely excluded. In the *Transvaal* and *Orange Free State* the franchise is explicitly restricted to whites, all adult white males who are citizens have the right to vote. *The Union* safeguards the Cape franchise by making any alteration of it dependent on two-thirds majority of both Houses of Parliament, sitting together, but it provides that only persons of European descent shall sit in Parliament, and assigns to the Cape Province a proportionate representation in the Assembly on the basis of its European voters only. The coloured and native voters are left out of the reckoning. The South African Act thus marked a decided set-back to the principle of racial equality in political matters.

Efforts are now being made even to deprive the natives in the Cape Province of the vote and participation in the elections to Parliament.

The most glaring expression of social discrimination is in the disproportion of money spent upon native education. A special tax for native education is enforced in South Africa. The natives do not object so much to this tax as such as to the principle upon which it is imposed; that is, that the native is the only section of the population specially taxed for his own education, whereas he has also to pay for the education of the European and coloured sections of the population. Even under the present conditions very little money is being appropriated for the cultural development of the children of native workers. For instance, the Bishop of Pretoria has recently been forced to state publicly that " more money was spent to build one high school for the white children of the bourgeoisie in the Transvaal than on the whole native educational system in the province."

In this respect figures speak more eloquently than words; therefore, we will quote the report of the *Native Affairs Commission* (1923) which glaringly shows the disparity in the amounts levied in direct taxation on the natives and the proportions spent for the education of their children.

(1) *Transvaal :* Native population 1,219,845, or 72.34 per cent. of total population.

Amount from Poll Tax	400,000	pounds sterling
Amount from Pass Fees	350,000	,, ,,
Amount spent on Education ...	56,000	,, ,,

(2) *Orange Free State:* Native population 325,824, or 61.69 per cent. of total population :

Amount from Poll Tax ... ... 86,000 pounds sterling
Amount spent on Education ... 5,000 ,, ,,

(3) *Natal:* Native population 953,398, or 79.24 per cent. of total population :

Amount from Hut Tax ... ... 270,000 pounds sterling
Amount spent on Education ... 32,000 ,, ,,

(4) *Cape:* Native population 1,519,939, or 59.26 per cent. of total population :

Amount from Hut Tax ... ... 175,000 pounds sterling
Amount spent on Education ... 170,000 ,, ,,

All of the above described facts briefly portray the misery, degradation and want to which 5½ million black toilers in South Africa have been reduced by means of arms, terrorism and bloodshed in the name of bourgeois democracy and the civilising mission of British imperialism.

II.—BRITISH EAST AFRICA

The partitioning of East Africa was begun about 1884 and completed within ten years. By 1890 the territories now known as Uganda, Kenya and Nyassaland came under British domination, while Tanganyika fell into the hands of the Germans. Because of the territorial position of this once-German colony, which lies between Kenya and Uganda on the North, and Northern Rhodesia on the South, the proposed Cape to Cairo railroad, which has been the dream of British imperialists ever since the days of Cecil Rhodes and Chamberlain, met with set-backs.

The German imperialists at that time were the greatest rivals of the British. They vigorously opposed the idea of such a valuable commercial and military railroad passing through their territory. Thanks, however, to the last imperialist war, Tanganyika has passed into the hands of Great Britain under a mandate of the League of Nations. This now gives Britain a solid continuous expanse of territory extending from Anglo-Egyptian Sudan in the North to the Cape of Good Hope in the South, and provides her with the possibility of effecting the railroad schemes as well as the establishing of air-routes.

The total area of the territories now comprising British East Africa is about 688,000 square miles, or seven times the size of England, with a native population estimated as about 10,957,634. There is also a European population of about 12,000, most of whom are farmers, Government officials and missionaries, as well as 67,978 Asiatics, chiefly East Indian and Arab traders.

The climate of East Africa, unlike that of the West Coast, enables Europeans to become permanent settlers in these colonies. This factor has greatly influenced the land policy that has been pursued by British imperialism in these territories. The plantation system has become the predominant form of agricultural exploitation in contradistinction to peasant production, which is widespread throughout British West Africa.

1. *Land Robbery.*

Thanks to German imperialism extensive plantations have been developed in Tanganyika by white capital and black labour. On the basis of this pre-war agrarian policy the British settlers have been able to continue the same plantation system, but their greatest difficulty to-day is the question of guaranteeing an adequate supply of labour. The same situation exists in Kenya, where the British colonial government, in order to solve the problem, has adopted the scheme of expropriating all of the fertile land in the highland regions from the natives, who have been driven into the barren lowlands.

It has been estimated that more than 10,000 square miles of table-land has been given to some 12,000 British farmers, while 5,000 square miles of unfertile territory has been set aside as *Reserves* for over 2,000,000 natives. In Kenya even this high-handed method of land robbery has not solved the labour problem. So, in order to find a way out, the Government has imposed special taxes known as the *Head and Poll* tax on the natives, along the same line adopted by the bourgeoisie of South Africa. It is hoped that in this way the natives will be forced to leave their *Reserves* and seek employment on the plantations of the Europeans in order to find the money to pay their taxes. Furthermore, whenever there is a great shortage of labour, taxes are increased until the situation is relieved. Natives who voluntarily go and offer their services to the whites are, however, exempted from paying the increase.

All males over the age of 16, as well as widows, are liable to the *Head and Poll* tax, which ranges from 10 to 16 shillings per annum. In 1924 the natives produced agricultural crops to the value of 546,000 pounds sterling. Yet they had to pay taxes to the amount of 876,000 pounds, of which sum 516,000 pounds was derived directly from *Hut and Poll* tax, and 250,000 from Customs. Thus the natives had collectively to go and earn 320,000 pounds from European employment in order to pay the Government. After securing their tax money they had to prolong their terms of " contract," so as to get an extra amount of money to buy food and clothing.

According to Sir Percy Girouard, a former Governor of Kenya, " *taxation is the only method of compelling the natives to leave their Reserves for the purpose of seeking work.* Only in this way can the cost of living be increased for the natives. It is on this that the supply of labour and the price of labour depends." This opinion was re-echoed by all of the European farmers who gave evidence before the Native Labour Commission in 1912, and as a result the Commission, which was composed of a British judge, three em-

ployees of the Government, two Christian missionaries and four
representatives of European commercial interests, recommended
that the natives be taxed on the one hand, their Reserves cut down
on the other, and in this way force more and more of them to go
into the labour market. As was to be expected, these recommendations have been put into effect.

2. Labour Exploitation

In order to get the labourers in the East African colonies, two
methods of recruiting have been resorted to : (1) official, and
(2) private recruitment.

Through the former method, pressure is brought to bear by the
Government officials on the chiefs, who are expected to supply
a certain number of able-bodied men to work for the Government
as well as for private individuals from time to time. With respect
to the other system, the private recruiters are known as labour
agents—quite a respectable term for slave dealers ! After obtaining
a licence from the Government, for which they pay a small fee,
they are at liberty to go into any province and comb it for workers.
These slave raiders are generally assisted by the native " touts,"
who act as guides.

Labour bureaus have also been established in various parts of
East Africa in order to facilitate recruiting. The largest of these
agencies are the *Fort Hall Recruiting Association* and the *Kisumu
Labour Bureau*, both of which are located in Kenya. Most of the
large estates in East Africa are situated in districts far removed
from densely-populated native areas, so that they are unable to
obtain from local sources all the labour they require. The labour
recruiter is therefore the link between the employer who needs
labour and the natives in their villages.

All male natives between 15 and 50 are liable for registration.
The percentage of those employed in Kenya in 1927 was 38.8.
Next to the Belgian Congo, which is notorious for its brutality to
the Negro workers, Kenya has more natives under European
employment than any other country in Africa. Last year some
27,000 labourers were recruited in Tanganyika territory alone,
for plantations and other big employers of native labour. About
30 licensed recruiters were employed in order to secure these
labourers.

This system of forced labour is legalised by the Legislative
Councils of the East African colonies. Violation of these slave
laws amounts to a criminal offence, punishable by imprisonment
and even flogging.

The first application of the official policy of forced labour for
private purposes was in 1919. Prior to this time, native labour
was exclusively used for Government purposes ; as, for example,
the building of roads, railroads, bridges and other forms of public
undertakings. However, shortly after the appointment of General

Northly, Governor of Kenya in 1919, the question of forcing the natives to work for private enterprises was raised in the Legislative Council in that colony.

During the course of the debate on this question, Lord Delamere, the leader of the European colonists, said : " We have got to come to legal methods and force the natives to work. I hope we may rely on the Government for assistance." Speaking on behalf of the Government, Northly replied : " I believe that our duty is to encourage the energies of all communities to produce from these rich lands the raw products and foodstuffs that the world at large, and the British Empire in particular, require. This can only be done by encouraging the thousands of able-bodied natives to work with the European settlers for the cultivation of land. . . . "

Later on the Governor, in a written communication addressed to the *European Farmers' Association*, stated that the official policy of the Government was: " The white man must be paramount— for the good of the country and for his own welfare he (the native) must be brought out to work. . . . Our policy, then, I believe, should be to encourage voluntary work in the first place but to provide by legislation to prevent idleness."

A few days after this declaration had been published the Chief Native Commissioner for Native Affairs, in the name of the Government of Kenya, issued another infamous document known as the " *Northly Land Circular.*" It stated " *that it is in the interests of the natives themselves for the young men to become wage-earners and not to remain idle on the Reserves for the large part of the year. The native authorities (chiefs and headmen) are therefore to exercise all lawful and proper influence (?) to induce young men to go into the labour market. It is also their duty to encourage all unemployed under their protection to seek labour on the plantations.*" The Circular further stated " *that where farms are situated in the vicinity of a native area, women and children should be encouraged to go out for such labour as they can perform.*"

Within a few months after these instructions had been issued to the native chiefs, 70,000 women and 150,000 children were assigned to European farms in Kenya. A campaign of recruitment spread like wildfire. Throughout Kenya Government officials organised labour armies of children and shipped them off to plantations. In *Kyambu District* the Commissioner issued a special circular appealing to the European planters, in which he announced that " *I shall be glad if any coffee growers who may like to employ these children will write his name thereon, stating the number required, the time for which they may be needed.*" (Buell—" Native Problem in Africa."—Vol. I., p. 334).

In summarising the native problem in Kenya we see that the black toilers are under obligation by law to perform two duties : (1) pay taxes, and (2) render compulsory labour for public and private purposes.

Similar conditions as those in Kenya also prevail in Uganda, where the principal enterprise is cotton growing. This crop is cultivated on extensive plantations controlled by British finance-capital through the British Empire Cotton Growers' Association.

Thousands of natives are recruited through the activities of the Uganda Planters' Association. This organisation pays its white agents 6 shillings for each Negro captured. After a few thousands have been collected they are then shipped off to plantations where they are forced to sign " contracts " to work for a certain number of months, during which period they are held as virtual slaves under the supervision of European overseers who ill-treat these labourers in the most shameful manner.

Forced labour is still utilised for the construction of railroads and roads in most of the provinces of Uganda. The average wage for a labourer employed by the Government is between 12 and 18 shillings a month. This is much higher than in Kenya where wages range from 6 to 10 shillings. In addition, the natives are made to work one month without pay for commercial purposes. There are over 20,000 such labourers at present employed in Uganda.

The same situation exists throughout Tanganyika, where forced labour has reached a very high state of development thanks to German imperialism, which laid the basis for it in pre-war days. In Nyassaland, unless a native can prove that he has worked for a white man for a certain number of months every year, he is made to pay a double tax.

In the few skilled occupations in which natives are employed in Tanganyika, wages are seldom higher than 20 shillings per month. But as a general rule the scale of pay depends upon the character of the work and the supply of labour at the time of the undertaking.

In July, 1930, delegates representing various associations of employers met at Kitali in Kenya and approved the resolution fixing the minimum wage for the signing on of labourers at 10 shillings a month. A second resolution was adopted discouraging farmers from making advances to natives entering employment, and suggested that the maximum should be no more than 10 shillings. It was further agreed that, in view of the present agrarian crisis, no rise should be granted to the native labourer unless he completed six months' employment at one continuous period in any given year, after which an increase of sixpence would be made if the labourer decided to remain the other six months of the year in the service of his employer.

As the workers in East Africa are recruited to a very considerable extent through native chiefs, it has become the policy of British political officials, such as District Commissioners, Superintendents of Police, etc., etc., to keep records of the chiefs and headmen so as to check up whether they are helpful or not. On the basis of this system, chiefs who fail to supply the alloted quota of men when called upon are either deprived of their chieftainship or otherwise a portion of their revenue is taken away from them until they comply with the demands of their imperialist masters.

The entire policy of British imperialism in East Africa has been fittingly summed up in the words of *Sir Charles Eliot*, the first Governor of Kenya : " The interior of the Protectorate of Kenya is a white man's country, *and it were hypocrisy to deny that white interests must be paramount and that the main object of our policy and legislation is to found a white colony.*" ("East Africa and Protectorate," pp. 105 and 310). This, however, was nothing original. It was merely the reiteration of Britain's imperialist policy in Africa which was formulated by Chamberlain, who, addressing the House of Commons on August 6th, 1901, on the question of forced labour and taxation, said : " In the interests of the natives themselves all over Africa, we have to teach them to work. . . . Suggestions have been made in the debate that it would be wrong to tax the natives. I do not agree at all. It would not for a moment be considered wrong to tax them on the ground that they were receiving benefits for which they pay their share of the cost. It is only suggested that it is wrong when there is the ulterior result that the native will have to work to obtain the money to pay the tax. Why should that which is right in itself be wrong because incidentally it will have a result which I venture to say is also right ? For if by these indirect means we can get the natives to undertake industry, we shall have done the best for them as well as for ourselves."

This policy has been consistently carried out by all of the Governments of British Imperialism, whether Conservative, Liberal or " Labour."

In order to tighten up its stranglehold over East Africa, British imperialism intends to amalgamate the colonies described above into one East African empire, towards which objective the " Labour " Government has stated its policy in two White Papers published in 1930.

III.—BRITISH WEST AFRICA

West Africa is divided into three parts under the domination of Great Britain, France and Portugal. Here we will deal with the British section, which comprises the colonies of Nigeria, Sierra Leone, Gold Coast and Gambia. Together they are about seven times the size of the United Kingdom with a native population of over 25 millions. Because of the tremendous economic importance of these colonies, we find the natives subjected to the same methods of robbery as in other parts of Africa. Up to a few years ago peasant production was widespread. This was due to the bad climate, which made it impossible for Europeans to settle there during the early days of colonisation, as they had done in East Africa. Modern science and engineering has transformed these colonies. Finance-capital is pouring into industry and agriculture with the result that the natives have been more and more expropriated from their lands. The Government is aiding the capitalists by means of taxation.

1. *Political Domination.*

Politically, the administration of British West Africa is in the hands of some 5,000 English officials, who rule directly, and in some instances indirectly (as in the case of Northern Nigeria), through native chiefs and petty black officials. The system of government prevailing throughout British West Africa can be placed under two heads : (*a*) *Crown Colony*, and (*b*) *Protectorate.*

Under the former the legislative and executive departments of the Government are under the domination of administrators known as Governors, who are appointed by the Secretary of State for the Colonies with the approval of the Crown. Under the protectorate system the Governor has absolute power ; however, the actual administration of government is carried on indirectly through native chiefs who are either appointed or approved of by the local administrators, known as Commissioners or Residents. The majority of these native chiefs are merely tools of the imperialists.

Neither of the two systems affords the toiling masses of African natives any voice in the political affairs of their countries. For example, the colonial parliaments known as Legislative Councils are composed largely of Government officials, such as the heads of various administrative departments of the State. The unofficial members are recruited from the British nationals, who represent banking, trading and shipping interests. Here and there one may find a few native members on the councils. These, however, are not the representatives of the working class, but of the native-petty-bourgeoisie and the landlord elements (chiefs and tribal headmen). Whenever the imperialists are opposed by bellicose chiefs or " left " petty-bourgeois intellectuals, they easily win them over by conferring a knighthood or some other form of imperialist decoration upon them, as well as appointing them members of the inner circle of oppressors by nominating them to seats on the various Legislative Councils.

By maintaining a majority of official members on the Legislative Councils, the governments of West Africa are always able to put through any enactment without popular opposition. However, when delicate situations arise, which require a certain amount of careful manœuvring in order to hide the mailed first of British aggression, the local administrators use the chiefs as agents through whom they extort taxes and demand labour out of the workers and peasants.

This policy of operating through native chiefs has become one of the most effective methods of subduing the toiling masses of West Africa.

This form of *Indirect Rule* was first introduced in Northern

Nigeria about 1900 by Sir Frederick (now Lord) Lugard, who at that time was the leader of the military expeditions which subdued the Fulani Emirates.   Since then this policy has become the method of ruling throughout the Protectorate of British West Africa.

2. *Land Robbery*

By annexing the lands, either as *Crown Lands* or *Public Lands*, the British administrators have completely reduced the Emirs (chiefs) to absolute dependence upon them, and as a result of this these black lackeys are now compelled to carry out whatever they are instructed to do.   Their emoluments are entirely in the hands of the British overlords, who could depose them at will as provided for by the *Appointment and Deposition of Chiefs Ordinance*, thus bringing their parasitic existence to a premature end.   In short, the whole policy of British imperialism in West Africa, like India, is to base itself upon the semi-feudal and other reactionary elements.

The principal functions which the native chiefs perform at present are those of labour recruiting agents and tax gatherers.   Whenever there is a shortage of labour the foreign plantation owners and mining companies, as well as State Departments acting through the provincial governments, order the chiefs to provide the required quota of labourers.   Thanks to the tribal institutions of the West African peoples, which generally conferred all sovereign power of the tribe in the person of the chiefs, and as such made them the custodians of all lands, they, especially in Nigeria and the Gold Coast, are still in a position to wield a great amount of influence over the broad masses.   These renegades exploited their prestige to the fullest extent by issuing orders calling upon all able-bodied men to leave the villages and go to work for the Europeans.

In the territories where the peasants refuse to obey the chiefs, as has frequently occurred in the Protectorate of Sierra Leone and Southern Nigeria, the Government simply steps in and by levying direct taxes on native huts, landholdings, agricultural produce and live stock, achieve their objective, namely, driving thousands of Negroes into forced slavery annually.   With respect to taxation in territories where Indirect Rule has been applied, the revenue is collected through native treasuries and divided between the chiefs, the tax collectors and the central government.   Among the 10 million black Moslems of Northern Nigeria these taxes are known as the *Hariji* and the *Gangali*.   The former is levied upon the farming population, while the latter is imposed on the pastoral tribesmen.   The rate is about one shilling per head for cattle and sixpence for smaller animals.

3. *Forced Labour*

In order to get the money to pay these taxes, the natives must do one of two things : (1) go to work for some foreign capitalist, or (2) borrow from the banks and native money-lenders.   In this way the imperialists are able to create a " free " labour market and thereby get labour for their plantations and mines, while the Government gets its taxes and the banks and other usurous elements interest on their loans. This, in brief, gives us a classical picture of the way these capitalist blood-suckers exploit the West African masses. In order to help in robbing the peasants of their lands by means of expropriation and taxation, the British utilise the chiefs. As a reward for their services these lackeys are permitted to deduct a certain portion of the taxes collected.

In West Africa forced labour can be divided into two categories : (1) *Forced compulsory labour for Government* and (2) *compulsory labour for private purposes.* As far as the Africans are concerned, there is no difference between these two systems ; for under both they are reduced to virtual slaves.

(a) *Government Use.*—Thousands of able-bodied men are used by the Government, for constructing roads, bridges and railways. All the railroads of West Africa are built, owned and operated by the Government, which pays its labourers on the average of 20 cents per day. Besides these workers there are some 30,000 miners employed by the Nigerian Government in working its coal mines. They get 25 cents for underground work and 18 cents for surface work. Native labour is also largely used for porterage. It has been estimated that over 86,000 porters, as well as 206,000 coolie-labourers, are in the Government's service in Southern Nigeria. Large contingents of porters are also employed in the Protectorate of Sierra Leone, and Gambia, where railroad and motor transportation is still in a backward condition. Porterage is one of the most devitalising forms of human exploitation, for the porters are made to carry heavy loads for hundreds of miles through dense forests and mud-covered roads.

(b) *Private Use.*—The following interview of a Nigerian mine-owner, which appeared in the journal," West Africa," gives a clearcut picture of the policy of the British imperialists towards native labour for private use. " They (the natives) are taxed annually by the Government, and in many cases they realise that the easiest way to pay such taxes is to work for the money required instead of selling goats or farm produce. The Government is certainly doing all it can reasonably be expected to do in assisting us in the matter of labour."

The following figures represent the approximate number of natives employed in the basic West African industries : In the Gold Coast there are about 10,000 miners employed by the Ashanti Goldfields Co. and other foreign concerns. The average wage is about 20 cents per day for 10 or 12 hours. There are over 30,000 miners in the tin industry in Nigeria. They receive about 1 shilling per day for 12 hours' work. Over 4,000 workers are employed in the manganese industry at the rate of 20 to 35 cents per day, while in the diamond mines the total number of workers in 1929 was 1,750.

According to the census of 1921, there were 20,000 wage earners in Northern Nigeria and 62,000 in Southern Nigeria. There were also 3,000 natives employed in the native administration of the Northern Province, and 86,000 porters as well as 206,000 coolie labourers in the Southern Province. The Government railroads operating in Northern Nigeria employed 6,360 natives. There are some 21,000 Nigerians in the Government service of the Southern Province.

The average wage of these workers, according to the character of their occupation, is between 30 shillings and 60 shillings per month.

The Annual Colonial Report (1929) issued by the Sierra Leone Government describes the labour situation in that colony as follows : " Unskilled labour in the colony and protectorate is easy to obtain. The wages paid average about 1 shilling or 24 cents per day.

" There is in the protectorate a system of communal labour which is performed by the natives as a form of tax payable to the chiefs. Such communal labour is called up in accordance with native customs or works of a public character, e.g., road-making, construction of native-built (mud) houses, but a system of payment for such labour is now being gradually introduced.

" The demand for skilled labour is met by skilled artisans trained by various Government departments of missions."

When the new harbour at Takordi in the Gold Coast was being constructed two years ago (1928), more than 6,000 natives were especially recruited from the villages and forced to do unskilled work.

The labour situation in West Africa has become such an international scandal that even the imperialists and their agents have had to admit its widespread practice.

For instance, Kathleen Simon, the wife of Sir John Simon, the British Liberal, in her book entitled " *Slavery*," states that : " ALMOST EVERY COLONISING GOVERNMENT TO-DAY IS EXACTING FORCED LABOUR FOR WHAT IT CALLS PUBLIC WORKS. VARYING PERIODS FROM 24 TO 60 DAYS A YEAR ARE EXACTED FROM THE FORCED LABOURERS; AGAIN, VARYING RATES OF PAY ARE ADOPTED. INDEED, IN A LARGE NUMBER OF CASES NO PAYMENT WHATSOEVER IS MADE."

We again find a confirmation of this in the official report on West Africa of Mr. Ormsby-Gore, former Parliamentary Under-Secretary for the Colonies, who, writing on the question of forced labour in the British West African Colonies, states : " The supply of voluntary labour for the latter purpose (road and railway construction) has always proved inadequate in Nigeria, and recourse is had to compulsory or ' enlisted '—sometimes called political—labour for these essential public works and services. All the railways and most of the roads in Nigeria have involved the use of this compulsory labour."

Domestic slavery existed in Sierra Leone up till recently. In 1929 the Supreme Court of Sierra Leone declared the institution of slavery illegal. But this was merely a political gesture, in order to create a mask behind which the representative of British imperialism at the League of Nations was able to manœuvre during the inquiry held on slavery in 1930, when a commission was appointed to investigate slavery and forced labour in Liberia

4. *Agricultural Labour.*

Within the past few years British capitalists have begun to develop large-scale plantations throughout West Africa. This has influenced the former land policy pursued by the Governments of the Colonies. The present tendency is to expropriate the lands from the natives and to turn the peasantry into a landless class of wage earners, enslaved on the plantations of the white overlords, as has been done in the East African colonies of Kenya, Uganda, Nyassaland and Tanganyika Territory, and the Belgian Congo.

In Nigeria the Government is working hand in hand with the British agricultural companies, which are dominated by the banks. The chiefs and the big native landlords are also giving active support to this new land policy, because their economic interests are identical with the foreign oppressors. They are the most reactionary elements throughout West Africa.

The standard of living of the agricultural workers is much lower than those engaged in the mining industries and transportation. For example, there are more than 20,000 labourers on some of the plantations in the Cameroons. The average wage is 10 cents for labourers and 30 cents for native overseers and foremen. Thousands of natives are also employed by European timber concessions in the Benin-River Territory. These workers are mercilessly exploited by the contractors who force them to work six months at a time before they are entitled to receive pay. During this period the workers are advanced the worst quality food in the company stores and at the end of six months the total of the advances made is deducted from their pay. As the result of this system the workers invariably find themselves indebted to the companies, which compel them to work another term under similar conditions. This system of peonage is most widespread among the timber regions of Southern Nigeria and the Cameroons.

The agrarian crisis, intensified by the monopoly rôle of finance-capital in agriculture, is creating universal pauperisation of the peasantry. Thousands of peasant producers have already abandoned their farms without any means of livelihood. If we take the conditions of the Gambian farmer to illustrate the point, we at once see the desperate economic position of these Africans. The average peasant cultivates 1 to 2 tons of ground nuts per year,

which fetch £5 per ton on the local market, thus making a total
income of £7 10s., while his living expenses amount to the following : rice during planting season, £1 16s. ; ground nut seeds for
planting £1 4s. Hut tax 4 shillings, poll tax 6 shillings. Cost of
living for 365 days at 1 shilling per day, £18 5s., making a total
of £21 15s. for living expenses as compared to an income of
£7 10s. Thus the West African peasant's expenses exceed his
income by £14 5s. annually. In order to augment the family
budget and make ends meet the entire family—father, mother and
children, are forced to seek employment in the open labour market,
which is unable to absorb them to-day. The alternative is to fight
for the overthrow of imperialism or to starve. The toilers are
beginning to follow the road of struggle which we will describe
elsewhere.

What with the tremendous fall in prices of farm products, increase
in value of manufactured commodities and imported foodstuff,
additional taxation and the application of more ruthless methods
of usury by the banks and money-lenders, general discontent is
being created among the toiling masses of West Africa. This
has already led to an open revolt in Nigeria in December, 1929,
during which 30,000 peasant women made an attack on the British
bank and trading companies in the south-eastern province of that
country.

IV.—French Africa

The French possessions in Black Africa are :

(1) *French Equatorial Africa*, commonly known as *French Congo*.
—This comprises one of the largest colonial possessions of French
imperialism. It covers an area of 975,635 square miles with a
population of 3,127,707 (census 1926). The Europeans number
about 2,502. These are largely political administrators, soldiers,
missionaries and representatives of mining, agricultural and other
commercial interests of the French bourgeoisie.

The territory was divided into three colonies up to 1919.

		POPULATION.			
Colonies	Area Square Miles.	Men	Women	Boys	Girls	Total
(1) Middle Congo	1,0,331	212,035	261,447	118,862	106,409	698,753
(2) Ubangi-Shari	207,997	350,800	377,594	174,349	163,701	1,066,444
(3) Gabum	121,893	126,840	161,388	51,524	49,147	388,899

In 1920 the Chad Territory, which was formerly a part of
Ubangi-Shari, was made a separate colony. It covers an area of
495,414 square miles and has a population of 923,611 natives,
composed of the following : men, 331,011 ; women, 317,259 ; boys,
116,491 ; and girls, 158,850.

The principal towns of French Equatorial Africa are Libreville in Gabun, Brazzaville in Middle Congo, Bangui in Ugangi-Shari and Fort-Lany in Chad.

Administration.—The entire Equatorial region is under the administration of a Governor-General, assisted by a secretary-general and a council. The Government has its headquarters at Brazzaville. Each of the four colonies described above is under the direct supervision of a Lieutenant-Governor, who has financial and administrative autonomy over the colony of which he is in charge. The Lieutenant-Governors are all directly responsible to the Governor-General of the entire territory.

(2) *French East Africa.*—The French possessions of East Africa are:

(a) The *Island of Madagascar*, which covers an area of 241,094 square miles with a population of 3,621,242. This includes the inhabitants of the islands of *Mayotte* and *Comoro*, two other possessions under the domination of France. The racial composition of the population is made up as follows: 18,040 French; 11,359 Europeans other than French; 3,591,943 Malagasy natives. Of the native population in 1925, 1,024,109 were males; 1,177,726 females; 1,374,266 children under the age of 15.

Administration.—*Madagascar* is ruled by a Governor-General, together with an economic and financial council, composed of 24 French and an equal number of natives. The French members are the representatives of commercial, agricultural and industrial companies with interest in the islands, while the native members are the representatives of the chiefs of the villages, who elect them to the council.

(b) *Mayotte and Camoro Islands.*—These have a combined population of 119,305, including 804 Europeans. Mayotte alone covers an area of 140 square miles and has a population of 12,674 (census 1925).

(c) *Reunion.*—This island has been in the possession of France since 1643. It covers an area of 970,000 square miles and has a population of 186,637, of which 180,694 are French, 628 East Indians, 1,963 natives of Madagascar, 1,626 Chinese and 411 Negroes.

The administration is in the hands of a Governor, assisted by a privy council and an elected counsel-general. The island is also represented in the French parliament by a senator and two deputies.

(d) *French Somaliland.*—This is on the African mainland between the Italian colony of Eritrea and British Somaliland, in the north-east of the continent. It has an area of 5,790 square miles and a population of 56,059, the majority of whom are Negroes. In Djibouti, the seat of Government, the population is 8,366, of whom 345 are Europeans (190 French) 3,428 Black Somalis and 238 Sudanese, 356 East

Indians, 109 Jews, 3,336 Arabs and 208 Donakils. The total non-European population is about 8,012.

Administration.—The territory is administrated by a Governor, assisted by a council.

(3) *French West Africa.*—The French West African possessions are as follows :

POPULATION 1926

Colonies	Area Square Miles	EUROPEANS French	Foreign	Natives	Total
(a) Senegal ...	74,112	330,057	1,593	1,313,637	1,719,399
(b) Guinea ...	89,436	1,135	1,127	2,093,726	2,185,424
(c) Ivory Coast ...	121,590	1,410	204	1,722,931	1,846,135
(d) Dahomey ...	41,302	737	147	978,725	1,020,911
(e) French Sudan ...	360,331	1,453	336	2,633,163	2,995,283
(f) Upper Volta ...	142,820	388	37	3,259,722	3,402,967
(g) Mauritania ...	154,400	178	101	288,905	443,584
(h) Niger ...	463,200	253	7	1,218,457	1,681,917
(i) Dakar and Dependencies	—	2,488	718	36,946	40,152
Total ...	1,247,191	338,099	4,270	13,526,212	15,335,772

Administration.—All of the above territories are administrated as a single political unit under a Governor-General, assisted by a council. The Government has its headquarters at Dakar. Each of the colonies is under the direct supervision of a Lieutenant-Governor, who is responsible to the Governor-General. Strong military forces are maintained throughout the territory. At present there are about 15,000 natives and 3,000 European soldiers, together with an armed police force of 5,000.

(4) *Mandated Territories.*—The former German colonies in Central and East Africa which were captured during the war and placed under Class C mandates by the League of Nations gave France the larger portions of Togoland and Cameroon. The other portions of these colonies were assigned to Great Britain.

(a) *French Togoland* lies between the British colony of Gold Coast on the West and the French colony of Ivory Coast on the East. The total area of the entire territory of Togoland is 33,700 square miles. France administers two-thirds or 21,893 square miles of this territory. The entire population is about 726,208, of which number 245 are Europeans.

(b) *French Cameroon.*—The French portion of Cameroon covers an area 166,489 square miles. The population is 1,874,683, of whom 647,341 are men, 690,866 women, and 548,886 children. The Europeans number 1,570 of whom 1,233 are French citizens.

1. *Labour Conditions*

Now that we have described the distribution of the French colonial empire in Africa, it is necessary for us to examine the economic and social conditions of the native population in these territories. The conditions of these masses are determined by the economic needs of French imperialism at this present state of the world capitalist crisis, which is beginning to affect the industrial life of France itself. What are these economic needs ? Briefly, (1) the development of colonial markets in order that they might be able to absorb some of the over-produced commodities of the French industries ; (2) the creation of greater opportunities for the investments of French finance-capital, and (3) to increase the cultivation of certain agrarian products in order to make France independent of other raw producing countries. Coupled with this economic factor, is the military. We shall attempt to show that in both these respects—economic and political—French imperialism has subjected the black population in its territories in the most brutal form.

2. Land Robbery and Taxation

In order to carry out its " civilising " mission two methods are applied by French imperialism : (1) expropriation of the peasantry from the land and (2) compulsory labour. By means of expropriation the Government accomplishes two purposes at the same time. On the one hand it has been able to grant great concessions to French companies for the development of cocoa, rubber, cotton, etc., etc., and on the other—to provide these plantations with cheap labour.

The workers that are assigned to the plantations are organised into squads and sent into the forest to collect rubber, monioc and other produce, for which they are paid at the rate of four and five francs per month.   Each worker is allotted a certain task and failure to accomplish this within a specified period of time means flogging and sometimes death, for the lives of the Africans are entirely in the hands of the European overseers.

In those regions of West Africa where the climate serves as a barrier for permanent colonisation of the agents of French imperialism, the plantation system gives way to peasant production. This, however, does not prevent the French imperialists from robbing the natives. This is accomplished through taxation. The peasants are forced to work season in and season out in order to find money to pay the tax gatherers. The chief allies of the imperialists are the native chiefs, who take a percentage of the taxes paid in to the Government treasury.

The standard of life of the natives in these colonies is very low, due largely to the miserable wages paid to them on their plantations. Those who still " own " lands are also hardly better off. What with the primitive methods of cultivation, to which are added frequently droughts, and the invasion of insect pests and taxation, these toilers are unable to provide enough nourishment for themselves. This widespread condition of malnutrition produces great apathy, and leads to diseases and epidemics. Their French masters nevertheless declare these black slaves the laziest beings in creation and have no hesitancy in "rationalising" their labour power by means of the whip. It is no uncommon sight to see thousands of natives toiling under the most devitalising tropical weather, hot sun or heavy rains, and standing over them armed guards with whips made of animal hide.

3. *Economic Exploitation*

It has been estimated that the French colonial mining companies produce minerals valued at more than 100 million francs a year. France gets from her colonial mines about 10 per cent. of her whole production. 90 per cent. of this amount comes from North Africa and Indo-China. French West Africa nevertheless possesses a tremendous abundance of mineral wealth. So in order to develop these resources the French Minister for the Colonies has embarked upon a new policy in West Africa. In order to induce the French bankers to invest their money in the development of the mineral resources of the Equatorial region the Government has pledged itself to undertake the recruiting of labour by its own agents so as to supply the various concessions held by the French companies. On an average between 800 and 1,000 workers are delivered to the companies every month. Thanks to this assistance by the State the French companies, despite the present world crisis, are able to declare millions of francs profit every year. For example, the *Equatorial Mining Co.*, which had a capital of 7,500,000 francs when it began operations five years ago, has now increased it to 20 millions of francs. The same thing can be applied to the mining company of the Congo, which has increased its capital from one million to 23 millions within a decade. The *Shangha Oubanghi Co.*, which had a capital of 12 million francs in 1911, increased the sum to 26 millions within ten years. There are about 40 such companies operating in the Equatorial region, all of which are making tremendous profits as a result of intensive exploitation of the labour power of the blacks.

This has resulted in the wholesale depopulation of villages. The Government is therefore attempting to introduce Indo-Chinese workers to relieve the pressure on the natives. But these imported workers are also beginning to join with the blacks against their overlords. Recent unrest among these Asiatic workers has compelled the French to curtail immigration. Those that are already in Africa are now being repatriated to Indo-China.

4. *Preparing For War*

Finance-capital is rapidly pouring into the development of railroad construction in French Equatorial and West Africa. The railroad development in these countries is being pushed forward with phenomenal rapidity. The economic reasons for this have already been enumerated above. However, it is necessary to emphasise the military aspect of these undertakings, because it shows the workers in France, as well as the blacks in Africa and the entire international proletariat, the imminence of another imperialist war, and a war against the Soviet Union. What do the facts in Africa show ? Four missions have recently carried out investigations on the possibilities of constructing a great railroad across the Sahara, from Algeria on the Mediterranean to the Niger River in Equatorial Africa. With the completion of such a railroad the report submitted to the Minister for the Colonies points out that half a million black soldiers could be transported quickly to the Mediterranean for service in Europe in the event of war or a proletarian revolution in France. The Commission further pointed out that the route to be undertaken should be over the western route because it was cheaper than the central and eastern schemes earlier proposed. The cost will be from 3,180 million to 4,185 million French francs. The railway should be built and worked by the Compagnie Nationale du Chemin de fer " Trans-Saharien," of which the French State, the French African colonies, the French railway and steamship companies, the North African Railways should be the shareholders for one-third, and the public the remainder. The Company's capital should amount to 150 million francs and 4 per cent. bonds should be issued, guaranteed by the French State.

According to the Paris *Depeche Coloniale et Maritime*, M. Doumergue, the French President (and a former Colonial Minister) delivered at Algiers, during his visit in 1930, a speech foreshadowing the construction of the " Trans-Sahara Railway " in the near future.

The *Depeche Coloniale et Maritime* " attaches much importance to this statement."

Furthermore, it is no accident that this Trans-Sahara railroad project was inaugurated by Tardieu at the time when he was Minister of Public Works. To-day this fascist minister occupies the Premiership, in which capacity he has assured his imperialist masters that no stone will be left unturned to push forward the railroad plans.

Another important railroad project recently carried out by French imperialism is the building of the Congo-Atlantic railroad from Brazzaville to Pointe Noire. In order to accomplish this project thousands of natives are being forced into service, hundreds of miles away from their homes. The line is 520 kilometres and will cost 1 milliard francs.

This is one of the most disintegrating influences on the tribal institutions of the natives. Between the years of 1921 and 1925 the territory of the Upper Volta furnished the railways with nearly 49,000 labourers. In 1924 the Upper Volta colony in addition employed 312,814 natives for other purposes. Because of the great difficulties which the Government experiences in recruiting

c

these labourers, due to the low wages and high death rate, the most brutal methods are resorted to.

Londres, the French journalist, in his book " *The Land of the Black*," describes the method of railroad construction in Equatorial Africa as follows :

" I have seen how railroads were built in other places. I have seen how special equipment and materials were prepared beforehand for the laying of the road. But here the Negro is used instead of machinery, instead of everything else in fact. He takes the place of the machine, the motor-lorry, the crane. And were it only possible he would be used instead of explosives too !

" In order to shift a barrel of cement weighing 260 lbs., the Batignolle Construction Co. uses as its equipment a stick and heads of two Negroes. I found here two other very modern instruments—the hammer and the pick. In Mayombi we intend to dig a tunnel with these instruments !

" The Negroes died like flies. Of the 8,000 that came to Batignaloes only 5,000 were soon left, and then 4,000 and later 1,700. New recruits had to take their places. But what was happening among the Negroes ?

" As soon as the whites made preparations for the road the cry of ' Machine ' went up everywhere (this is how the Negroes call the railroad). The Negroes knew that the whites had gone to find more people to build the railroad. They ran away. ' You yourselves taught us '—they told the missionaries—' that we must not commit suicide, but to go on the " machine " means death.' They sought refuge in the forests of the Chad Coast in the Belgian Congo. In districts that were once inhabited by man the recruiting agents found only the chimpanzee. Can you build the railway with monkeys ? We started to hunt the Negroes. Our men caught them as best they could with the help of lassoes, etc. We put ' collars ' on them, as they are called here. The human material recruited in this way was not of the best. . . . The death-rate increased—' We must reckon with a loss of six or eight thousand people,' said Governor General Antonette, ' or give up the railroad.' But the number of victims was greater. To-day it already exceeds 17,000, and there is still about 200 miles to go ! . . . We are woodcutters in the human forest."

Work away from home is one of the most disintegrating influences on the tribal institutions of the natives. Between the years of 1921 and 1925 the territory of the *Upper Volta* furnished the railways with nearly 49,000 labourers. In 1924 the Upper Volta colony in addition employed 312,814 natives for other purposes. Because of the great difficulties which the Government experiences in recruiting these labourers, due to the low wages and high death rate, the most brutal methods are resorted to in order to force them into service. The healthiest and most able-bodied men and women throughout the entire Equatorial territory were commandeered for railroad work, which is done without the aid of machinery, and as a result the mortality is exceedingly high, as the workers cannot stand the intensive rationalisation, speed-up, poor quality of food and unsanitary conditions under which they are forced to live. It has been estimated that over 25,000 natives have already perished on the Congo-Ocean railroad.

The population of French Equatorial Africa has decreased from 7,500,000 to 2,500,000 within a period of 10 years. The causes for this are largely due to forced labour conditions and the intensive militarisation of the youth. Thousands of able-bodied men die annually from consumption and other diseases contracted while serving in the army in France. The natives are not only unaccustomed to the European climate, especially its rigorous winters, but they are housed in unsanitary barracks and provided with the cheapest quality food.

V.—BELGIAN AFRICA

The history of Belgian colonisation and exploitation in Africa is notorious. As oppressive as other imperialist countries have been in Africa, Belgium has surpassed them in its brutality to the native population. It is therefore necessary for us to give a brief sketch of the Congo and its historic background in order that readers might be better able to appreciate the way in which the country has been robbed and the natives enslaved.

The *Belgian Congo* is one of the largest colonial possessions in the world. It covers an area of 918,000 square miles, which is about *eighty* times the size of *Belgium*. The native population, which is chiefly of the Bantu stock, numbers about 8,500,000. The white population in 1927 was 18,169, of whom 11,898 were Belgians, 844 English, 443 Americans, 1,368 Portuguese, 981 Italians, 128 Russians (Whites), 138 Swedish, 523 French, 317 Dutch, 228 Swiss, 478 Greeks, 127 Luxembergers, 34 Danish, 31 Norwegians, 320 Spaniards and 622 of other nationalities. The colonisation of the Congo began in 1876 as a personal venture of Leopold II. With all the hypocrisy and lying characteristic of the imperialists the Belgian monarch assured the world that his interest in the Congo was to " open to civilisation the only part of our globe where it had not yet penetrated." Furthermore, the Congo mission promised " to protect the natives in their moral and industrial well-being, to advance science and education, spread the Christian religion, abolish slavery and the slave trade." Let us see what extent these imperialist robbers have fulfilled their pledge to the natives.

A few years after Leopold turned his attention to Africa he discovered that the country possessed tremendous natural resources. His first act was to declare this vast territory his personal property, and in order to exploit the resources he entrusted the country to a number of concessionaries, reserving for himself half of the stock in each Congo Company. The concessionaries divided the territory

into provinces which were administrated by the directors of each
company. They adopted a uniform policy of taxing the natives,
not in money but in produce. While there was abundance of
ivory and rubber to be had, blacks were made to supply the labour.
Armies of men, women and children were mobilised and dispatched
into the forests to collect these products. In order to see that the
work was effectively carried out a native army was organised under
European officials. Failure to bring in the allotted quantity of
ivory and rubber resulted in a punishment by flogging. As the
natives were forced to work in the jungles unarmed, and a great
distance away from their villages without any provisions of food
or shelter, they died out like flies. This situation became so disgraceful that other imperialist powers, seeking an opportunity of
gaining some of the African spoils, demanded Leopold to let them
share in the exploitation of the Congo. As a result of this pressure
Leopold granted four major concessions to French, English and
American capitalists in 1906. The American Congo company
exploited rubber ; another company minerals in Katanga; a third
inaugurated a railroad project, while a fourth concern interested
itself in mining and agriculture. After Leopold had indebted himself with over 20 million dollars and guaranteed that the sum of
50 million francs be paid him in addition to 45 million francs, which
he promised to use " for the embellishment of the cities of Brussels
and Antwerp," together with an annuity to his royal successors,
he turned the Congo over to the Belgian State. Thus ended the
humanitarian project of Leopold and the first phase of the enslaving
of the Negroes of the Congo.

Beginning where Leopold left off, the Belgian bourgeoisie vied
with each other in annexing as much of the territory as possible.
Aided by *Social Democracy*, they assured the Belgian workers that
the Congo was overflowing with richness of every sort ; it is the
biggest reservoir that the country can have at its disposal. Without
it Belgium would stifle. Having bribed the upper strata of Belgian
workers into support of their imperialist schemes by assuring them
that their standard of living would be raised in proportion as the
country is developed, they set about the re-organisation of the
Congo. It was placed under the administration of a Governor-
General and the supervision of a Minister for the Colonies and a
council of 15. The minister and 8 members of the council are the
the special appointees of the King. The Governor-General is
assisted by a number of Vice-Governor-Generals who administer
various sections of the Congo. For administrative purposes the
Belgian Congo is divided into four provinces : (1) *Katanga* (capital
Elizabethville) ; (2) *Congo Kassai* (capital Leopoldville) ; (3) *Equator*
(capital Coquilhatville) ; and (4) *Eastern* (capital Stanleyville).

A military force of over 20,000 native soldiers under 198 European
officers and 228 European non-commissioned officers are stationed
throughout the Congo. Natives are made to serve in the army

for seven years. The Government also maintains an armed territorial force of 10,000 men. In this way, whenever the toiling masses revolt against the brutal oppression imposed upon them, the military forces are called in to suppress the uprisings. The policy of the Belgian Government in the Congo is one of armed imperialist dictatorship.

The second stage of exploitation began after the war. The Belgian bourgeoisie by turning its attention to the Congo was able to recuperate the economic life of the metropolis which had passed through the devastating effects of the war. In order to stimulate national interests in the Congo, King Albert paid a visit to the country in 1930, on which occasion, true to the traditions of Leopold, he said in his public speech that " the Congo is an integral part of our country. Belgium is conscious of its high mission of civilising the Congo and in its own interests must not neglect any means nor retreat before any sacrifice in order to assure the progress of this splendid colony." Albert need not have any fears about the " civilising " mission of his bourgeoisie. For we can already see the extent to which these exploiters have ravished the country. For example, the Union Mine Company of Katanga, according to the Boston News Bureau, is one of the largest copper producing mines in the world, surpassing Chile, which has hitherto been the greatest copper producing country in the world, by 2,436,500 pounds. This copper has been produced by an army of native miners amounting to nearly 20,000. These workers, like the agricultural labourers, are recruited through force. The entire male population of the villages are drafted into labour battalions at the point of the bayonets of Belgian and native soldiers and marched to the various mining camps. There they are compelled to work for a certain number of months for wages which average between 4 and 5 francs per month. Out of this miserable pittance the workers are compelled to provide their own food. Housed in vermin-infested shacks, they soon become infected with disease, to which large numbers of them succumb. Because of the terribly low wages for which these miners work, the representatives of the company of the recent Copper Conference held in America in 1930 were able to assure the delegates that, despite the tremendous fall in the price for copper, the Belgian Company can continue to defy world competition and make money. The profits of this company increased £2,700,000 in 1929 as compared with £2,260,000 in 1928. Exclusive of copper mining, tin, gold, diamond, coal and radium industries have reached a high stage of development. The industrial proletariat is estimated at about 500,000. A large number of these workers are also permanently employed on the railroads, which are by far more highly developed than those in Belgium. For instance, the Bengula-Katanga railroad employs about 60 white workers and 10,000 Negroes. The Francuki-Bikama railroad, over which a large percentage of Congo copper is transported to its European market, has a staff of 260 whites and 6,000 natives. There are at present 8,000 natives employed in the construction of a new line on the Matadi-Leopoldville railroad.

Hundreds of natives are also employed on the docks as stevedores, sailors, boatmen, while the majority of the labour for the electrical and power stations in the Congo are Negroes. As a result there is quite a large body of skilled native labour in the basic industries of the country.

In the sphere of agriculture, Belgian and other foreign companies have invested millions of pounds. For example, one of the biggest concerns is the *Huileries du Congo Belge*, a branch of Lever Brothers and United Africa Company. It holds monopoly of the palm oil industry with plantations and factories in Leverville, Alberta and Elizabetha, which employ over 30,000 natives at the rate of four francs per day.

The whole project of industrialisation in the Congo has created a serious problem, for the population is underfed, without necessities, and therefore unable to survive the intensive application of rationalisation. In order to fight against the inhuman conditions imposed upon them, the workers have attempted to organise and take up the offensive against the imperialists, but in most cases these strikes have been suppressed.

The Belgian Mandate.—After the war, Belgium secured a mandate over the densely inhabited highlands of Urandi-Ruanda, which was a part of former German East Africa. Belgium demanded this booty as a reward for her participation in the last imperialist scramble for colonial markets.

Since Belgium has assumed administration over this territory the natives have lived in a state of perpetual hell. All their lands have been stolen from them. What remains is insufficient to provide food. As a result famines are sweeping every year over the country, claiming hundreds of victims. The natives, faced with the situation of struggling for actual existence, revolted against the Belgian Government, under the slogans of "Land—or death to every white man." But the Belgian troops suppressed the uprisings. A wholesale slaughter took place. The troops shot down over 40,000 natives. They burnt down the natives' huts ; hundreds of thousands of Negroes fled to the colony of Uganda, but the British Government ordered the soldiers of the King's East African Regiment to arrest the refugees and deliver them back to the Belgina Government, which shot every one of them. According to the official report of the Congo medical service for 1930, the Roman Catholic missionaries, known as the *White Fathers' and Sisters'* station, in the *Ruanda district* were forced to attend to 806,429 natives who were wounded or ill as a result of the famine and punitive measures carried out by the Belgian Government. A description of the uprising which took place in Ruanda will be given in the next chapter—dealing with struggles.

VI.—PORTUGUESE AFRICA

Portugal was one of the oldest colonising powers in Africa.   Her possessions in this part of the world are :—

	Colonies.	Area.	Population.
(a)	Cape Verde Islands ...	1,480 ...	149,783
(b)	Guinea	13,940 ...	289,000
(c)	Principe and St. Thomé		
	Islands	360 ...	59,005
(d)	Angola	484,800 ...	4,119,000
(e)	Mozambique	426,712 ...	3,120,000

(1) *Military Rule.*—Mozambique, or Portugese East Africa, is divided into three political units : (1) the Province of Mozambique, (2) the territory under the Mozambique Company, and (3) the territory under the Nyassa Company.   Each of these provinces or divisions has its own Governor, together with a council composed of Government officials and representatives of various commercial and agricultural interests.   Cape Verde and the other islands are administered by Governors assisted by local councils.

Portugal maintains military forces in each of her colonies.   There are about 4,000 native and Portuguese soldiers in Mozambique ; 5,000 in Angola, of which 3,602 are natives ; 135 natives soldiers and 10 white officers are stationed in St. Thomé, while 247 soldiers, of whom 143 are natives, are garrisoned in Guinea.   With the aid of these military forces Portugal enslaves the black population in her colonies.

(2) *Slavery on Cocoa Plantations.*—Historically speaking, the Portuguese imperialists were among the first slave traders in Africa. True to their traditional occupation, they are still the vilest oppressors of Negroes in Africa.   The worse forms of slavery exist in all the Portuguese possessions, especially on the islands of *St. Thomé* and *Principe,* as well as on the mainland colonies of *Angola* on west and *Mozambique* on the east coast.

(a) *St. Thomé and Principe.*—These two tiny islands situated off the coast of West Africa are of tremendous importance to Portuguese imperialism as raw material producing countries.   Over £1,500,000 worth of cocoa is exported from these islands to Europe annually.   There are no peasants on the islands, for years ago the Portuguese have completely annexed all the lands, which are considered exceedingly fertile, and have converted them into extensive plantations.   As the imperialists and their families do not work on plantations themselves, it has been necessary to provide labour to do the cultivation.   Portugal, like other colonial exploiters, naturally resorted to forced labour.   But as the indigenous populations of these islands are small, the labour supply was very limited. They, however, soon found a solution.   The plantation owners, most of whom resided in Europe, compelled the Portuguese imperial

Government to instruct their representatives in Angola to co-operate with the colonial planters to force the blacks to go to the islands to work. This the Government willingly consented to in order to enable the home bourgeoisie to develop raw materials independent of their rivals in other imperialist countries.

Labour agents who are nothing else but slave raiders are permitted to go throughout Angola and recruit as many Negroes as the plantations need. These slave dealers are always escorted by soldiers, so that when the natives resist the bayonets are always at hand to bring pressure to bear on the poor unarmed blacks.

(3) *Corruption of Officials.*—The slave trade has reached tremendous proportions in Angola. To-day there are special recruiting companies with regular agents throughout the country. Government officials also actively participate in this human traffic. It is a well-known fact that Portuguese officials vie with each other to go out to Angola in order to enrich themselves on the spoils of the slave trade of the Negroes.

Professor E. A. Ross, an outstanding American sociologist at the University of Wisconsin, who investigated conditions in the Portuguese territories, describes the corruption among the European officials in the following way : " The Colonial service is far less a career than formerly and the official is much keener to make money quickly. This latter observation is emphatically confirmed by a thoughtful merchant in one of the towns. In his judgment none of the Portuguese office-holders come out with any other thoughts than gain. Neither officials nor traders create anything ; they only squeeze. . . . Why should they look ahead and plan to promote the economic upbuilding of the country ? They do not care for the country, they never expect to settle there. They care not even for the future of the Government which they represent. Their controlling thought is to make money before another is given their place. They realise it is theirs ' to make hay while the sun shines.' "

Referring to the actual method applied by officials in robbing workers, Dr. Ross says : " In practice forced labour works out as follows. A labourer works for the coffee planter, and at the close of his term of service the planter says, ' I can't pay you anything, for I have deposited the stipulated wage for you with the Government ; go to such and such an office and you will get your pay.' The worker applies there and is told to come around in a couple of months. If he has the temerity to do so, he is threatened with the calaboose (prison) and that ends it. It is all a system of bare-faced labour stealing. They think that the planter has really paid for their labour, but that the official does them out of it."

(4) *Methods of Recruiting Labour.*—Over 80,000 natives have been exported to the islands within a period of ten years. After the slaves have been collected in gangs in Angola they are chained

around the neck and marched for hundreds of miles from the inter'or to the coast, where they are auctioned off to the plantation owners, after which they are packed together on the filthiest ships and taken away to St. Thomé and Principe. Some ships take as many as 800 during a single voyage.

The average price for a strong adult Negro is between £30 to £35. Boys and girls fetch about £15 to £20. The lot of these miserable beings is beyond description. To avoid the charge of exaggeration we will quote evidence from the writings of bourgeois travellers who have visited Angola and investigated conditions. Mr. Joseph Burtt, a representative of the British chocolate manufacturers, the Cadbury Company Ltd., is describing the misery of the natives during their journey from the hinterland to the coast, says: " A dealer once admitted that if he got six out of every ten natives to Bihe he was lucky, but sometimes only three survived the journey. This was due not only to the physical strain of tramping nearly seven hundred miles under miserable conditions, but to the fact that the captives were often so hopeless that they refused to eat. Many who were seen to be of no value received a mortal wound, or were left to die of hunger. Cases of incredible cruelty were constantly witnessed. It was not long before we found skeletons and shackles. These shackles are blocks of wood, in which an oblong hole is hewn to admit the hands and feet. A stout peg is then driven through the side, dividing the ankles or wrists, and making withdrawal impossible. They vary in size and shape. I saw some intended for women's hands, with a fork for the neck. A long heavy pole is sometimes used, and must be a terrible instrument attached to the neck. In the gully of a dry stream-bed, where we stayed to rest, a few yards from where we sat, and under the side of an overhanging rock, we saw the decomposing corpse of a man. Hard-by lay a small basket, a large wooden spoon, a native mat, a few filthy clothes. The dead man lay on his back, with his limbs spread out, probably as he had died, left hopelessly weak by a gang going down to the coast. Another skeleton lay within a few yards, making five we had seen in a few hours' march."

Mr. H. W. Nevinson, another investigator, writes : " The path is strewn with dead men's bones. You see the white thigh-bones lying in front of your feet, and at one side, amongst the undergrowth, you will find the skull. These are the skeletons of slaves who have been unable to keep up with the march, and so were murdered or left to die."

Some years before the war a very interesting case known as *Cadbury against Standard Newspapers Company Ltd.*, in which Cadbury brought an action for libel against the newspaper company, came up before the Birmingham Assizes. In the course of the trial evidence was given to the effect that the Cadbury Company was offered the sale of a cocoa plantation in St. Thomé and among the assets included in the property were " 200 black labourers, for £3,555." This glaring fact again indicts the Portuguese imperialists and their apologists. They were selling human beings at £18 per head !

Lord Carson, one of the lawyers engaged in the case, in describing the situation in the Portuguese colonies, said : " Slavery ! Have you ever heard at any time of the world's history (and that is a broad statement) of worse conditions of slavery, have you ever heard of conditions more revolting, more cruel, more tyrannous and more horrible than what has been deposed to as regards the slavery in San Thomé ? Men recruited in Angola, women re-cruited in Angola, children recruited in Angola, torn away against their will from their homes in the interior, marched like droves of beasts through the hungry country, and when they are unable to walk along for a thousand miles to the coast, shot down like useless dogs or useless animals, and the others brought down to be labelled like cattle and brought over to San Thomé and Principe, never again to return to their homes. Three and a half years' life at the start until they are acclimatised is an average life of these people, and when their children are born, just as the calves of a cow or the lambs of the sheep, they become the property, not of their parents, but of the owners."

Angola.—What exists on the islands also prevails on the main-land of Angola. Forced labour is also used on the sugar cane plantations for private purposes as well as for road and railway construction and other forms of public works. It is no uncommon sight to see hundreds of men and women, as well as children be-tween the ages of 12 and 15, working on the roads under soldiers and armed overseers. Even skilled artisans are under compulsion to work for wages fixed by the various employers' associations supported by the Government. At the present scale of wages a skilled worker has to labour four months in order to get enough money to pay his taxes. The labour situation in Portuguese West Africa has become such a scandal that even an openly im-perialist controlled body like the League of Nations has been forced to make a protest to Portugal as a gesture of support to the memorandum addressed to that body by the workers of Angola. The memorandum states that : (1) owing to the miserable wages fixed by the Government on the one hand, and the high taxes imposed upon the workers on the other, the Government has been compelled to use force to get skilled labourers to work for the imperialist concerns ; (2) that on account of the unsanitary con-dition of the ships used to convey natives from Angola to San Thomé and Principe Islands, hundreds of these poor victims die during the mid-passage.

To these charges the Portuguese Minister for the Colonies, Brigadier-General Eduardo Marquis, makes the impudent excuse that " of course there may be misuses in our colonial administration, as there are in all other colonial administrations, but the Government does all that is possible to avoid them." What a defence for slavery !

The following excerpts from the report of Professor Ross confirms the truth of the abuses to which the natives are subjected :

(1) " Six years ago ten men from his village were taken away on a train by soldiers to work and they have never been seen since."

(2) " Another (native) testified that six years ago twenty-five or thirty men from his village were taken to San Thomé and had never been heard from since."

(3) " The village chief declared that eight years ago the officials took from his people eighty-four persons and forty-four from the people of the adjacent chiefs. Nothing has been heard from them nor of them. He supposes that they are at San Thomé. After three years the two chiefs were called by the local authorities and told to be patient. ' We will send for these men and have them brought back.' But none have ever come back."

(4) " Four years ago a large number who were tax delinquents were sent to San Thomé and have never returned."

(5) " They (the natives in Village No. 5) state that six years ago five requisitioned by the Government from this village were taken to San Thomé and never came back."

(6) " We met here the chief of five villages, including this one, with a total population of about 2,500. Six years ago a hundred of them were taken away to San Thomé and none ever came back."

The Mozambique Convention

Similar conditions as those on the west coast exist in Mozambique in East Africa.

In 1928 the British South African Government signed a treaty with Portugal known as the *Mozambique Convention*. By the terms of this treaty South African capitalists, especially the mining campanies, are entitled to import Negroes from the Portuguese colony of Mozambique, to supply the labour force in the mines. The reason why the mine operators had to turn to Portuguese East Africa was because the white South African farmers by imposing certain restrictions on the native labour prevented an adequate recruitment of Negroes within the Transvaal. Since the Convention has come into existence, thousands of blacks have already been imported into the Union and enslaved in the mines. The terms of treaty provide for the employment of Portuguese Negroes in the Transvaal mines as follows :

1929	... ...	100,000 natives
1930	... ...	95,000 ,,
1931	... ...	90,000 ,,
1932	... ...	85,000 ,,
1933	... ...	80,000 ,,

The conditions under which these slaves live are vile beyond description. For as badly off as the indigenous population of South Africa is, the Negroes brought in from the Portuguese territories are a thousand times worse. They are made to work for about a year and a half, after which time they are so broken in health because of the absence of normal living conditions, together with bad food, that they are no longer able to work. They are then loaded into freight trains and shipped back to Mozambique and a new contingent is then recruited and brought to take their places in the mines.

British imperialism cannot escape its responsibility for this state of affairs. It is not only morally, but legally reponsible for this situation as well as slavery in West Africa, for according to the terms of an agreement entered into between Great Britain and Portugal, England has assumed the responsibility of protector and defender of the colonial possessions of Portugal against foreign enemies.

However, neither the British nor Portuguese Governments or their colonial officials will ever remedy the present situation. For this is the only way in which imperialism draws super-profits from colonial exploitation. Only the organised might and revolutionary forces of the millions of natives in these Portuguese colonies will be able to drive these imperialist oppressors away from the plantations into the sea.

VII.—Spanish and Italian Africa

(a) *Spanish.*—The area and population of the Spanish colonies in Black Africa are as follows :—

	Colonies.	Area.	Population.
(1)	Spanish Guinea	10,036	140,000
(2)	Fernando Po and Annobon		
(3)	Corsico, Great and Little Elobey	795	22,846

The population of Fernando Po alone, the most important of the islands, is 20,873, of whom 300 are Europeans, including 30 British. The administration of the Spanish colonies is under a Governor-General assisted by sub-governors for various political units.

(b) *Italian.*—Exclusive of Tripolitana and Cyrenaica in North Africa, Italy controls the black territories of Italian Somaliland and Eritrea in North East Africa.

(1) *Somaliland* covers an area of 190,000 square miles and has a population of 900,000, of which 1,000 are Italians and the rest natives. The colony is ruled by a Governor who resides at Mogadiscio, where he is assisted by a Secretary-General and a military commandant.

(2) *Eritrea* extends over an area of 45,754 square miles and has a population of 402,793 natives. There are also 4,000 Europeans of whom 3,900 are Italians. The administration is conducted by a Governor, who resides at Asmara, a city with a population of 14,511 inhabitants including some 2,500 Europeans. A military garrison of about 5,000 native troops under the command of some 200 commissioned and non-commissioned Italian officers is maintained in the colony. There is also an armed police force stationed in the most important centres.

Labour Conditions under Spanish imperialism are no better than those found in other parts of Africa. For example, thousands of natives are recruited from the Negro republic of Liberia and shipped to the Spanish island of Fernando Po to work on the cocoa plantations under conditions similar to those in the Portuguese colonies. The recent International Commission on Slavery which investigated forced labour conditions in Liberia discovered that there existed an agreement between the Liberian and Spanish Governments, whereby slave dealers were permitted to hunt down Negroes in the interior of Liberia and export them to Spanish colonies. The Spaniards paid the Liberian officials a special tax on every Negro shipped out of the country. Very few of the labourers ever returned back to Liberia. Those who did not die during their period of " contract " were left stranded on the island, and having no money to pay their passage back home were forced to renew their agreement with the planters for another period of years. This process is repeated from time to time until the poor victim is relieved by death.

In the Italian colonies fascism rules with all the bloody ruthlessness that labour is subjected to in Italy. By means of bayonets and machine guns the population in Somaliland is forced to work for their dictators. A whole tribe was removed in 1930 from one section of the country to a new region in order to isolate them from neighbouring tribes whom it is charged they were contaminating with ideas of revolting against the Italian military regime. In order to solve the unemployment problem in Italy, the Government is annexing the lands from the tribes and turning them over to Italian colonists, who are being encouraged to migrate from Europe and settle in Africa instead of foreign countries. Through this policy Mussolini is conserving Italian man-power under the banner of fascism so that in the event of war he could utilise these white colonists together with the native population as a colonial army for European or African campaigns.

CHAPTER II

BLACK SLAVES IN THE NEW WORLD

BESIDES the 200 million Negroes estimated inhabiting the Continent of Africa, there are between 40 to 50 million Negroes scattered throughout the New World—the United States, the West Indies and Latin America. They are the descendents of the slaves who were brought from Africa to work upon the plantations and the mines in the territories which they now occupy. Therefore, unlike their black brother in Africa, the Negroes in the New World have had centuries of contact with the white capitalist civilisation. But like the Negroes in Africa, they are subjected to the same barbarous methods of imperialist plunder and exploitation.

I.—THE UNITED STATES OF AMERICA

Even in the United States, which the apologists for bourgeois democracy consider the "land of the free and the home of the brave," we find 15 million Negroes brutally enslaved. The story of the oppression of Negroes in the United States forms one of the darkest pages in the history of capitalism. In no other so-called civilised country in the world are human beings treated as badly as these 15 million Negroes. They live under a perpetual regime of white terror, which expresses itself in lynchings, peonage, racial segregation and other pronounced forms of white chauvinism.

The vast majority of the 15,000,000 Negroes in the United States are toilers—industrial workers and poor peasants. The bulk of them are still on the land, either as agricultural labourers, share croppers or tenant farmers. They live in certain sections of the Southern States, where they are so thickly populated that they form a sort of compacted territory of their own, known as the "Black Belt." Here the Negroes are in the majority.

There are some 219 counties in the South where the population is nearly half or more Negroes. The State of Georgia, which covers an area of 52,265 square miles with a population of 2,895,832, has the largest black population of any state in the American Union ; while the State of Mississippi, which is 46,865 square miles with a total population of 1,790,618, the blacks number 52.2 per cent. (census of 1920).

And, strange to say, it is in these thickly populated territories that the Negroes suffer most oppression. They are absolutely at the mercy of every fiendish mob incited by the white landlords and

capitalists. Bands of business and professional men make peri-
odical raids upon the black countryside, where they lynch Negroes,
burn homes and destroy the crops and other property belonging
to the blacks. In most cases of lynching the Negroes are burned
to death after their bodies have been soaked in gasoline, while
others are hanged from trees. On these occasions the entire white
community turned out to witness the bloody spectacles, which were
made " Roman Holidays."

White ruling class terrorism becomes so vicious at times that
entire Negro communities move away and seek new homes in the
North and other parts of the country where they are better able to
defend themselves. It is estimated that over two million Negroes
left the South for industrial cities during the war and post-war
period.

1. *White Chauvinism and the Labour Movement*

Race prejudice or white chauvinism is one of the chief weapons
in the hands of the capitalist class in order to oppress and enslave
the black workers. In the United States the working class is made
up of different nationalities and races which are grouped into white
and black. In order to prevent these workers from uniting together
in militant struggle against the bourgeoisie who rob them all alike,
the employers and their agents in the Labour movement (reformists
and social-fascists), encourage the workers to hate each other by
playing up racial and national differences.

As a general rule Negroes are not permitted to join the reformist
trade unions, which are under the control of social fascist leaders
like William Green and Matthew Woll, of the American Federation
of Labour. As a result of this policy of discrimination, the black
workers in the North, like those in the South, are compelled to do
the hardest and dirtiest work for the lowest wages. And in periods
of economic depression, such as the present, they are always the
first to be discharged from their jobs. With the seven million
unemployed in the United States to-day, the Negroes are feeling
its effects more severely than any other section of the working
class. Millions of them are now walking the streets of every big
city of the North and the rural districts of the South faced with
the spectre of starvation and death.

The only trade unions of America which admit Negro workers
on the basis of *full political, economic and social equality* are the
revolutionary unions affiliated with the Trade Union Unity League,
the American Section of the Red International of Labour Unions.
These unions are under the influence of Communist leadership
and conduct intensive national campaigns calling upon the black
and white workers to unite against the American bourgeoisie, and
their labour agents, the reformist trade union leaders of the
American Federation of Labour, as well as the socialists, whose
policy it is to divide the workers on the basis of colour in order

that they may be exploited more effectively. In this the capitalists have been fairly successful in the past, but the workers are now beginning to see the folly and danger of racial antagonism and are starting to unite into militant trade unions and unemployed councils, under the leadership of the Communist Party and the revolutionary trade union centre, the T.U.U.L.

2. *Southern Oppression*

The Southern bourgeoisie and landlords are largely the descendants of the former slave-owning class. They are the most oppressive of the American ruling class. Trained in all the vicious practice of chattel slavery, they torture and brutalise their workers in the most barbarous fashion. Living in constant fear of the Negro masses, the capitalists, who exploited them to the very limit, maintain a reign of fascist terrorism through the State apparatus (court, police, militia), as well as the Church. Some of the most active agents of the oppressors are the preachers, who go around the countryside stirring up racial hatred and mob law against the Negroes.

The most widespread forms of economic, political and social oppression of Negroes are : (*a*) peonage, (*b*) slavery, (*c*) lynching, (*d*) Jim Crowism.

Most of these terrorist practices against Negroes are perpetuated by specially created fascist organisations, such as the Ku Klux Klan, the American Legion, the Black Shirts, the Caucasian Crusaders, etc., etc. These organisations are supported by the bourgeoisie and reactionary middle class elements. They invade the sections where the Negroes live, burn homes and crops, kill off live stock, poison drinking water wells, murder and lynch unarmed men, women and children who dare to offer resistance to their pogroms.

A few words about each of these forms of socio-economic oppression :

(*a*) *Peonage.*—Peonage is the most brutal and demoralising form of economic exploitation. It has its basis in the rent and profit system which grew out of chattel slavery. After the Negroes were " freed," they had no land of their own or the means whereby to gain a livelihood, so most of them were compelled to remain on the plantations of their masters. Some of them sold their labour power for wages, while others entered into a sort of feudal contractual relationship which bound them to the land like serfs. The landlords allot a certain quantity of land to each black family, and supplied tools, seed and food to the tenants until the harvest has been reaped. The crop is then taken over by the landlords, who sell it and afterwards make an account to the tenants. The tenants are always given less than what the crop sells for, and in this way they continually find themselves indebted to the landlords. For example, if a Negro cultivated a hundred bales of cotton which fetched 600 dollars on the market, the landlord will present him with an account of 800 dollars for supplies alleged to have been rendered during the year, so even if the Negro paid the 600 dollars he would still owe the landlord 200 dollars, which he would be compelled to pay off by planting another crop under similar conditions as before. This is repeated year after year. Even if the Negro took the landlord to court his statement of the facts would not be believed, because the word of a white man cannot be refuted by a black. Furthermore, the Southern landlords are not only the overseers, bookkeepers of their plantations, but are the political dictators of the community as well, and when they make a statement it becomes the law of the court. It has always been the prerogative of the ruling class of the South to decide when the Negro workers should leave their service, or under what conditions they are bound. Negroes who rebel against these outrages and run away are hunted down by the police and other uniformed thugs, with the aid of bloodhounds which are especially employed for this purpose. They are brought back to the plantations and turned over to the landlords either as vagrants or as runaways.

Another method by which labour is recruited is through the chain gang. Whenever the landlords need labour they simply go to the local judge and arrange that the police be ordered to arrest the required number of workers. In this way whole communities of able-bodied blacks are commonly apprehended. All kinds of frame-up charges are made against them. When fined in court they have to agree to enter the service of the landlords, who pay a small fine for the opportunity to reduce the Negroes to servitude. In this way the judges and the police get the court fees, and the landlords cheap labour.

A brief account from one of the peonage districts is sufficient to illustrate this point. Passing along the street where a Negro had been mistreated by his white master, an observer inquired of the worker : " Why do you stand this ? " " That is just the damned trouble down here " responded the black, " I once complained to the court when another white man beat me. The man denied it and the judge, who believed his story, imposed upon me a fine which I could not pay, so I have to work out in the service of this man who was present in the court at the time and paid it in order to get the opportunity to force me to work for him."

Whenever there is a shortage of labour the Southern capitalists do not only resort to these repressive measures, but also commandeer the use of child labour. For example, by order of the white county superintendent (Memphis, Tennessee), 8,000 Negro students enrolled in schools of Shelby county were taken out of the school-rooms and placed in cotton fields during the season of 1930.

The " cotton recesses " affect only Negro students. Coloured schools are always closed until after the cotton crops are gathered. Negro rural schools in the South are run for an average of six months, with two suspensions, one for the planting and the second for the picking of cotton. White schools are open for the usual nine-month term. Compulsory child labour is widespread throughout the South.

(b) *Slavery.*—Thousands of blacks are still being held as slaves in the coal mines and on road construction work in the States of Alabama, Mississippi, Texas and Georgia. A law was enacted in the State of Florida in 1919 to the effect that, whenever a Negro is unable to pay his debts, he is to be imprisoned, and the jailer has the right to rent him out to a farmer until such times as the farmer is satisfied to release him.

There is a special law in Mississippi which makes it a criminal offence, punished by fines or imprisonment, for agents to enter the State and contract for labour. This law was enacted in order to prevent Negro tenants and agricultural labourers from leaving their masters, no matter how badly they are being treated or how high the wage offered by other employers outside of the State.

A white man by the name of Wilson, who owns a 7,000 acre farm near Greenwood, Mississippi, went into the county of Moxubee scouting for Negro farm labourers in 1930—he had signed up 25 coloured workers and had chartered two freight trucks for their transportation to Greenwood when the business men and plantation owners in Moxubee discovered Wilson's activities. They immediately organised a band of 100 men and drove Wilson out of the town. The Negroes who had dared to sign up to leave were stripped naked and most brutally flogged in public as a warning to other blacks never to attempt to migrate.

Investigations have disclosed the existence of large slave farms in the extreme Southern part of Florida. Over 5,000 Negroes have been collected from various parts of the State and lured away to toil in the turpentine camps, where they are forced to work day and night under armed guards. Life in these places are indescribable hell holes. The workers are huddled together in shacks, given a minimum amount of food of the worst quality, and denied the most elementary sanitary conveniences. Conditions are more primitive than in some colonial countries. As a result, disease is very rampant in these barbed-wire compounds. Hundreds of blacks die annually from starvation and exposure, while others meet a quicker and more welcome death at the hands of their cruel task masters.

(c) *Lynching.*—Hand in hand with peonage is mob rule, which expresses itself in lynchings. These outrages, although chiefly perpetrated in the South, occur in other parts of the United States of America.

Over 3,256 Negro farmers and workers have met their death at the hands of white lynching mobs between 1885 and 1930. Georgia heads the list of lynching States with a record of 441 Negroes and 256 whites during the period of 35 years. There is hardly a month which does not bring its tidings of this form of class outrage and racial terrorism.

The circumstances under which a Negro named Henry Lowry, about forty years of age, was lynched typifies the practice as it has developed in the United States. The story of this outrage was written on the scene of the lynching by a reporter of a capitalist newspaper, who describes the incident as follows :

" More than 500 people stood by and looked on while the Negro was slowly burnt to a crisp. A few women were scattered among the crowd of Arkansas planters who directed the gruesome work. Not once did the slayed beg for mercy despite the fact that he suffered one of the most horrible deaths imaginable. With the Negro chained to a log, members of the mob placed a little fire of leaves around his feet. Gasolene was then poured on the leaves, and the carrying out of the death sentence was under way.

" Inch by inch the Negro was fairly cooked to death. Every few minutes fresh leaves were tossed on the funeral pyre until the blaze had passed the Negro's waist. As the flames were eating away his abdomen, a member of the mob stepped forward and saturated the body with more gasolene. It was then only a few minutes until the Negro had been reduced to ashes.

" Even after the flesh had dropped away from his legs, and the flames were leaping towards his face, Lowry retained consciousness. Not once did he whimper or beg for mercy. Once or twice he attempted to pick up the hot ashes in his hands and thrust them into his mouth in order to hasten death."

A correspondent of the" Memphis News Scimitar," another Southern bourgeois paper, wrote the following description of the lynching of a young Negro worker in Tennessee.

" I watched an angry mob chain a Negro to an iron stick. I watched them place wood around his helpless body. I watched them pour gasolene on this wood. And I watched the men set this wood on fire. I stood in a crowd of 600 people as the flames gradually crept nearer and nearer to the helpless Negro. I watched the flames climb higher and higher, enclircling him without mercy. I heard his cry of agony as the flames reached him and set his clothes on fire.

" ' Oh, God ! ' he shouted. ' I didn't do it. Have mercy ! ' The blaze leaped higher. The Negro struggled. He kicked the chain loose from his ankles, but it held his waist and neck together against the iron that was becoming red with intense heat.

" ' Have mercy, I didn't do it—I didn't do it ! ' he shouted again and again.

" Soon he became quiet. There was no doubt that he was dead. The flames jumped and leaped about his head. An odour of burning flesh reached my nostrils. I felt suddenly sickened. Through the leaping blaze I could see the Negro sagging and supported by the chains.

"When the first odour of the baking flesh reached the mob, there was a slight stir. Several men moved nervously.

"' Let's finish it up,' someone said.

Instantly about twelve men stepped from the crowd. They piled wood on the fire that was already blazing high. The Negro was dead, but more wood was piled on the flames. They jumped higher and higher. Nothing could be seen now for the blaze encircled everything.

"Then the crowd walked away. In the vanguard of the mob I noticed a woman. She seemed to be rather young, but it is hard to tell about a woman of her type, strong and healthy, apparently a woman of the country. She walked with a firm even stride. She was beautiful in a way.

"The crowd walked slowly away.

"' I am hungry,' someone complained, 'let's get something to eat.'"

Thus ended another act of the great drama of American civilisation !

Of the ten lynchings which occurred in 1929, the last one took place in the State of Kentucky on Christmas Day—the occasion on which the bishops and priests and the other "holy men of God," who carry on a campaign of lies and slander against the Soviet Union, were chanting their hymns to their God and shouting " *Peace on Earth, Goodwill to Men !* ".

Since the beginning of 1930, 36 lynchings have already taken place. One of the victims was a Negro women about sixty years old, the mother of four children. The woman worked for a white farmer in North Carolina. He refused to pay her wages and she threatened to report him to the police. That same night the farmer organised a group of business men and landlords, led them to the woman's house and took her to a nearby field where she was hanged from a tree.

After the lynching of two Negroes, Shipp and Smith, at Marion, Indiana, pictures of their charred bodies were sold in the shops of the city of Terre Haute, where bloodthirsty capitalists bought these stocks up as souvenirs of "how to keep the 'niggers' in their place."

However, one of the most fiendish and atrocious outrages committed against a Negro worker occurred in Jacksonville, Florida, on Christmas Eve in 1930. A Negro youth by the name of *Timothy Rouse*, employed as an orderly in a municipal hospital, was accused of carrying on amorous relations with a white fellow-worker. The physicians at the hospital became so infuriated over the idea of a white woman being in love with a Negro that they called a meeting of the business men of the city who demanded that Rouse be immediately dismissed. Shortly afterwards the Negro was arrested and thrown into prison. A few days later a mob, headed by the petty bourgeois elements of Jacksonville, broke into the jail, placed the youth into an automobile and took him to the outskirts of the city where he was placed under anæsthetics and castrated by doctors who were part of the mob. The hooligans then returned to the city and ordered an ambulance to go to the spot where the victim was left and remove him to a Negro hospital. As usual the State officials, many of whom participated in the outrage, made no attempt to discover the culprits, giving as the excuse that the inhuman operation was performed " by unknown parties."

As barbarous as this outrage is, let it be known that Rouse is not the first Negro to be subjected to this form of atrocity. A number of similar cases occurred in other sections of the South, where the ruling classes—in their determination to prevent any relationship between the white and black workers, resorted to the most barbarous and savage assaults upon Negro men suspected of having any personal relationship with white women.

(d) *Segregation*—better known in America as Jim-Crowism, is the most widespread form of social oppression in the United States. Wherever Negroes live, whether in the North or South, they are segregated in their social relationships from the whites. This applies most generally in public utility service, schools, hospitals, recreation centres and other places of amusement, etc. In some States Negroes are not even allowed to ride in the same coaches with the whites. Wherever railroad companies agreed to permit them to ride, they are provided with small dirty wooden compartments, for which they have to pay the same fare as the white passengers, who enjoy the most up-to-date railroad conveniences. On Southern street-cars, Negroes get in and off from the rear while the whites enter from the front and have priority to the best seats. In those places where Negroes are admitted to the theatres they are forced to enter through back doors, and inside the theatres are huddled together in filthy balconies far removed from the stage.

Black workers are not permitted to patronise restaurants which cater to whites, neither are they allowed to use the same public bathing beaches or entrances to buildings as other people. Negroes are debarred from libraries, museums, art galleries, and other centres of culture. Very limited educational and cultural opportunities are offered to them. In most places they are compelled to send their children to separate schools, and, as is to be expected, the capitalist State expends by far more money on the education of white children than black, although the Negro workers are made to pay the same taxes for the maintenance of the public schools system.

A few figures will illustrate the marked disproportion in the educational budget for blacks and whites in the South:

South Carolina	(dollars) 60,12	for white child ;	5,90 for Negro
Georgia ...	„ 48,00	„ „	7,00 „ „
Mississippi	„ 32,57	„ „	6,00 „ „
Louisiana ...	„ 74,24	„ „	8,20 „ „
Alabama ...	„ 40,92	„ „	8,70 „ „
Arkansas ...	„ 32,23	„ „	9,00 „ „
Florida ...	„ 78,22	„ „	12,00 „ „

In the face of this marked discrimination for the education of the two races, one can easily appreciate the tremendous handicaps which the children of Negro workers and peasants are confronted with in acquiring education and culture. Nevertheless, through great personal sacrifices, the Negroes have themselves carried on the struggle to liquidate illiteracy.

(e) *Disfranchisement.*—Politically, Negroes in the South are completely franchised; this is done with open violence and terror. On election days there are armed white mobs, agents paid by the capitalist politicians to keep the Negroes away from the polls in the Southern States. Furthermore, certain enactments, known as the " Black Laws," have been incorporated in the Statutes of some States in order to more effectively deprive the Negroes of their political rights. These laws are chiefly based on property and educational qualifications. As the vast majority of Negroes are propertyless, and their standard of literacy is a matter to be determined by the politicians (Republicans and Democrats), it becomes very easy for them to be ruled off the ballot. During every election campaign in America, Negro workers who attempt to vote are openly shot down before the polling stations by armed thugs and gangsters, specially hired by the various capitalist parties to prevent the blacks from taking part in the elections. The *Republican, Democratic and " Socialist "* parties are all hostile to the Negroes. Only the Communist Party fights for their full economic, social and political equality, and champions the right of self-determination for the Negro masses who inhabit the *Black Belt.*

(f) *Ghetto Life.*—Wherever one goes in America one sees a striking similarity in the appearance of black communities derisively called " *Nigger Towns.*" The outstanding feature of these ghettos are their very unsanitary conditions. For the bourgeois politicians, although they compel the Negroes to pay the same amount of taxes as the whites, never spend any money to improve the standard of life among the black workers. Epidemics frequently break out in these black settlements, taking heavy toll among the workers, especially their children. The death rate among the Negro workers in America is in some cases 50 per cent. higher than whites. This is especially so in the case of contagious diseases, such as tuberculosis, typhus, etc.

Even in the North, where Negroes are supposed to be better off than in the South, they are still the victims of varied forms of social oppression. First of all they are isolated from the rest of the working class by traditional social codes imposed upon the workers by the bourgeoisie, in order to maintain an ideological influence over the white workers, who are taught to hate and despise their black comrades. Therefore, we find that the less class-conscious white workers, like the capitalists, have the tendency to consider the Negro workers as social outcasts—members of a pariah race.

II.—THE WEST INDIES

It has been estimated that there are about 10 million Negroes in the West Indies, which are a group of islands situated in the Caribbean Sea between North and South America. Collectively they cover an area of over 90,000 square miles.

1. Political Divisions

The islands are politically divided up into the following categories :

(a) *British.*—Britain controls the following colonies : (1) Jamaica, (2) Trinidad, (3) Barbados, (4) Windward Islands, (5) Leeward Islands, (6) Bahamas. These islands cover a total area of 28,600 square miles, with a population (in 1926) of about 1,500,000.

(b) *French.*—The islands under the domination of French imperialism in the Caribbean are : (1) Guadeloupe and Dependencies, which consists of a number of small islands, that collectively cover an area of about 688 square miles. The total population of the entire territories is estimated at 243,243 ; (2) Martinique : this island covers an area of 386 square miles and has a population of 244,482.

(c) *Dutch.*—The Dutch West Indies comprise the colony of Curacao and the islands of Bonaire, Aruba, Saba and St. Martin. The area of the entire colonies is 405 square miles, with a population of 53,000.

(d) *American.* The Caribbean possessions of American imperialism are Porto Rico and the Virgin Islands. (1) Porto Rico covers an area of 3,435 square miles. The population is about 1,299,809, of which number 351,062 are Negroes, (2) The Virgin Islands, formerly known as the Danish West Indies, have an area of 132 square miles, and a population of 26,051. Of this number 24,486 are Negroes.

2. Administration

(a) The British colonies are administered under the Crown Colony System. In each political unit there is a Governor assisted by a Legislative and Executive Council composed of officers of the State and representatives of commercial, shipping and agricultural interests. In a few colonies, such as Jamaica, Trinidad, Barbados and Grenada, there are a few elected members on the Legislative Council. These, however, are the representatives of the native bourgeoisie and the landlords. In Trinidad there is a Labour Party based on the trade unions with a few representatives in the Legislative Council and the Municipal Council in Port of Spain. The toiling masses of black workers and peasants of the West Indies have no voice in the Government. In the few instances where the franchise exists the property qualifications are beyond the reach of the working class. The British Government also maintains military forces in a number of these islands. One of the largest garrisons of white troops is stationed in the Island of Jamaica.

(b) The French Colonies are administered by Governors assisted by Councils. The Islands are also represented by Senators and Deputies in the French Chamber. The military forces, consisting of artillery and infantry, are maintained in both islands.

(c) The administration of the Dutch Colonies is in the hands of a Governor assisted by a Council, composed of a Vice-President and three members nominated by the Netherland Government. The centre of administration is in Curacao. The Governor is represented in the various islands by special political officers called Gezaphibbers.

(d) America administers Porto Rico by a Civil Governor, appointed by the President of the United States. The Governor has full executive power and is assisted by a Council composed of the heads of various Government Departments. The Legislature consists of two Houses, the Senate and Representatives.

The Virgin Islands are administered by a Governor appointed by the President of the United States. The natives have no representation except on the municipal councils maintained in the three islands of St. Thomas, St. Croix and St. John.

(e) Among other imperialist colonies on the American continent inhabited by Negroes are : (1) *British Guiana* in South America, (2) *British Honduras* in Central America, and (3) *Bermuda*.

British Guiana covers an area of 89,480 square miles, with a population of 306,844, including 9,700 aborigines (Indians). There are also 126,246 East Indians in the country; the balance of the population are mostly blacks.

British Honduras has an area of 8,598 square miles and a population of 48,584 Negroes.

The Bermudas are a group of small islands in the Atlantic, about 677 miles from New York. The total population is 20,801, of which 13,682 are Negroes.

3. *Labour and Social Conditions*

The Negro masses in the West Indies are just as viciously exploited as the natives of Africa or the black toilers in the southern parts of the United States of America. Their exploiters are not only the foreign imperialists, but the native bourgeoisie and the landlords, who are equally as ruthless in their suppression of the broad toiling masses as the foreign blood suckers. In no section of the Black World are class lines more sharply defined than in the Caribbean colonies.

After the abolition of slavery in 1834, the Negroes refused to continue to work on the plantations. The British Government, in order to save the sugar industry from sudden collapse, made grants of land to them on the basis of which a peasantry was developed. At the same time it was necessary to secure labour for the big plantations. So, in order to overcome this, East Indian immigration was instituted in 1845. Thousands of coolies were brought from India and indentured on the sugar cane plantations in the British colonies.

These workers were so badly misused that the Government of India was forced to protest to the Colonial Office, added to which the sugar crisis in 1917 caused by the competition between West Indian sugar and beet in the European markets forced the colonial planters to abolish the indentured system.

That is why we find a large section of the toiling population in the colonies of Trinidad and British Guiana are composed of East Indian coolies.

Since the war the policy has been to liquidate the peasantry and to concentrate all the lands in the hands of big native planters, absentee landlords and foreign corporations.

In this way the peasants are fast becoming a landless semi-proletariat, working part of the time on the land and another part in industry. The land problem is the biggest economic and political issue in the West Indies to-day. Everywhere the natives are in revolt against the big landlords and their governments.

In Cuba, Porto Rico, Haiti and San Domingo, American capital has been able completely to enslave millions of black workers on the sugar cane, coffee and tobacco plantations. In order to facilitate the development of these agricultural undertakings, thousands of natives are imported annually from Haiti and Jamaica to work on the sugar plantations of Cuba, Porto Rico and San Domingo.

In the British colonies of Jamaica, Trinidad and Barbados, British imperialism is as ruthless as American. Throughout all of the West Indies one is confronted with the shocking spectacle of whole populations living on the verge of starvation. In the rural districts we find thousands of pauperised, down-trodden natives, huddled together in company-owned barracks on the sugar plantations or scattered round the countryside in mud shacks. The social conditions among these victims of imperialism is hardly much removed from primitive life. Forced to labour long hours on the smallest pittance, the West Indian worker is scarcely able to provide himself with the most elementary necessities of life. Women and children are forced to go into the fields and labour in order to augment the family budget. The male agricultural workers receive about 40 cents per day, while women and children get between 15 and 30 cents.

In the larger British colonies, especially in Trinidad, where there is an extensive oil and asphalt industry, a well crystallised industrial proletariat has been brought into being with recent years. In the asphalt industry, which is a monopoly in the hands of the New Trinidad Lake Asphalt Company, Ltd., thousands of Negroes are employed to dig the pitch (asphalt) and to load ships at La Brea, the principal shipping port for this industry. These men receive an average wage of 50 cents per day, and live under terrible conditions.

The oil industry, controlled by the Royal Dutch Shell and Pearson's interests, is centred in the Southern section of the island. The vast majority of workers employed in the various oil-fields are Negroes. However, within recent years Hindu workers have been attracted to the industry.

Apart from the industries described, the marine workers form an important section of the West Indian working class. The bulk of sailors, longshoremen, boatmen, etc., in the West Indian ports are Negroes. The internal transportation system, such as railroads, streets-cars, buses and taxis are all operated by black workers. A few thousand Negroes are also employed in minor industries.

4. *The Agrarian Crisis*

The present economic crisis, due to the complete bankruptcy of the sugar industry, which is a reflection of the world crisis of capitalism, has reduced the West Indian toilers to a condition beyond description. Starvation and disease are causing havoc in depopulating entire sections of the population, especially in the rural districts of the islands.

We can imagine how badly off these people must be when the Church of England, which has for centuries aided the British imperialists to maintain their domination over the blacks, has been forced to appeal to the Imperial Government to aid the Negroes. However, we must not permit ourselves to be fooled by this ecclesiastical gesture. The Church, in making this appeal, is also trying to safeguard its own position, for much of its financial backing came out of the sweat and blood of the agricultural labourers, who have been taught to work hard, be obedient to their exploiters, have faith in the Christian God and food would always be guaranteed them. But the crisis is rapidly disillusioning these black slaves and arousing their class consciousness. Therefore, the religious dope peddlers are doing their best to direct the growing revolutionary spirit among the masses into safe channels by holding out promises of Government relief to them. According to " The Times " (1-7-30) the Bishops of the West Indies presented the following resolution to the Secretary of State for the Colonies in support of the Olivier Commission which investigated the sugar situation in the islands in 1929 :

" The Bishops of the province of the West Indies make strong representation to his Majesty's Secretary of State for the Colonies in regard to the destitution to which the labouring classes of the sugar-producing colonies are being reduced by the present crisis in the sugar industry. In view of the extreme gravity of the situation, they beg respectfully to press for the adoption by His Majesty's Government of the recommendations contained in the Olivier Report."

The Archbishop said the ministers of religion had passed that resolution because, in their judgment, " the conditions of the Negro labourers caused by the crisis in the sugar industry was rapidly developing into a situation of serious urgency. Their wage was deplorably small. The recent Sugar Commission, over which Lord Olivier presided, speaking of their wages as it existed before the incidence of the present crisis, stated that ' wages are already hardly sufficient to maintain more than a bare subsistence,' and gave the general rate of wages as from 1s. 6d. to 2s. a day for men and 10d. to 1s. 3d. for women. In this connection it was most important to remember that in Barbados and the Leeward Islands the great majority of the Negro labourers had not only to feed and clothe themselves and their families on this inadequate wage, but also to rent houses or keep their own houses in repair."

The Olivier Report also states that in St. Kitt's " *there was squalor and degradation among the great majority of the labouring classes.*" That statement applied to other sugar colonies besides St. Kitt's, and in many places little or nothing had been done since 1897 to improve these conditions " of squalor and degradation." " Their food was insufficient in quantity and quality, considering the nature of the work they had to do. A quite considerable proportion of these people of all ages and both sexes suffered from malnutrition. In the country district for the most part no baths or other sanitary conveniences were provided. This applied universally to estate villages and was largely true of other villages as well."

In consequence of this deplorable state of affairs, diseases prevailed which were preventable and curable, and were sapping the energy and efficiency of the population. Besides the unsanitary conditions prevailing among Negro labourers in the villages, the Olivier Report called attention to the unsatisfactory condition of factories " from the point of view of the health and safety of the workers employed in them."

These conditions would be made much worse unless something was done by His Majesty's Government to put the sugar industry on a basis of permanent stability.   The deputation wished to make its own quotation from the 1897 report, which was repeated in the Olivier Report : " The black population of these colonies was originally placed in them by force as slaves ; the race was kept up and increased under artificial conditions maintained by the authority of the British Government."

The deputation also supported all those statements of the Olivier Report which direct the attention of the Government to the inevitable effect of the present crisis of the sugar industry upon the condition of the Negro labourers ; as, for instance : " There would inevitably be pressure to reduce wages, which are already hardly sufficient to maintain more than a bare subsistence, and the added effect of this would further worsen the already unsatisfactory standard of health " ; and, they would add, the general bad social and economic conditions prevailing.   This result had already been produced.   Wages had been considerably reduced, and the communication from the Dean of Antigua stated that the labouring people in the island of Antigua are faced with starvation.

The deputation therefore urged with all respect to the adoption of the recommendations of the Olivier Report, since it was confident that any other method of tiding over the result of the present crisis as it affected the Negro labourers would produce a very serious disorganisation of the whole labour situation, from which the West Indian colonies would take generations to recover.

According to the latest reports, the situation has become so deplorable that the " Labour " Government, in order to avoid a general uprising of the toiling population, has been forced to appropriate a sum of money from the imperial treasury in order to provide work for the population in Barbados and British Guiana.   This can only be a temporary measure, for the situation cannot be remedied by such artificial methods.   The social-fascist politician, Lord Olivier, is again visiting these colonies, in order personally to aid the native labour misleaders and national reformists to keep the masses in submission by making them promises of establishing " prosperous " conditions in the near future.

5. *Forced Labour*

The same conditions which exist in the British colonies also prevail in the French islands of *Martinique* and *Guadeloupe*, where agriculture is the main occupation.   All of the large sugar plantations are owned by French companies, which make great profits by robbing the Negro workers, who receive a few francs per day.

The conditions which prevail in the Virgin Islands of the United States are most appalling.   The Negro workers hardly get more than two days' work per week, for which they receive an average wage of 35 to 50 cents.   Grim hunger stalks the land, taking its toll among the children of the poor.

Forced labour also exists in the West Indies.   Whenever there is a shortage of labour for public works the Governments of the various colonies, especially in Haiti, commandeer the services of the natives for the necessary labour. Nearly all the public roads have been constructed by forced labour gangs under the military supervision of the United States marines. In the British islands all kinds of repressive legislation, such as vagrancy laws, are enacted in order to enable the imperialist rulers to find a pretext to force the Negroes to work. Workers and peasants are arrested on all kinds of framed-up charges, thrown into prison and there assigned to chain gangs and made to build roads and do other forms of public work.

III.—LATIN AMERICA

In spite of the loud and pompous declarations about equal rights contained in all the constitutions of the Latin American Republics, it is, however, a fact that in the economic, social and political practice of these countries the Negroes do not enjoy these constitutional rights. The Latin American bourgeois ideologists lie when they say that all men are equal ; lie when they try to prove that there is no economic and racial discrimination against Negroes in Latin America.

There is hardly any country of Latin America where the Negro toiling population does not consider itself humiliated and insulted by the economic and social practices of the white ruling class.

The percentage of Negroes in these countries varies greatly. In Brazil there are nearly 10,000,000 Negroes, in Colombia, out of the total population of 3,000,000 (in round figures), there are more than 25 per cent. Negroes ; in Venezuela, Negroes and half-castes (Whites, Indians and Negroes) form nearly 70 per cent. of the population, the total number of which amounts to 3,026,878 ; in Cuba 30 per cent. of the population are Negroes ; in the Dominican Republic (San Domingo), Negroes form one-fourth of the population, the total number of which, according to the 1929 census, amounts to 894,660 persons ; in Panama, to 444,486 persons, 353,930 are Negroes and mongrels. In Peru, Ecuador and other countries, there are great numbers of Negroes, besides Haiti, where the number of whites is absolutely insignificant. In all of the countries in which the Negro population lives together with the whites, however, they suffer from all sorts of humiliation and insults. This refers to the Negro population as a whole, bourgeois, petty bourgeois and workers. But if we consider the Negro workers alone, the question becomes even more acute.

If the Negroes in liberal professions (petty bourgeois intellectuals) find it difficult to live owing to systematic persecution, one can easily imagine the terrible conditions of the Negro toilers, especially in view of the fact that they are more systematically denied the right to work in certain occupations. For example, highly-skilled Negro workers are compelled to work as unskilled labourers, because they are not given the opportunity to do the work they are able to perform.

The native-born Negroes throughout all the countries of Latin America drag out this miserable existence thanks to race hatred and superstitions. But there is still another category of Negroes in Latin America, who meet with even more vicious forms of oppression. We have reference to the emigrants.

For some time past the national bourgeoisie and the North American imperialists, in order to obtain cheaper labour power in Latin America, began to import into these countries large numbers of Negro workers from Haiti, Jamaica, etc. On the banana plant-ations of Colombia and Honduras, as well as on the sugar plantations of Cuba and elsewhere, practically all the farm labourers employed have been imported from Haiti and Jamaica. It is, indeed, difficult to imagine anything more inhuman than the conditions under which they live and toil. Deceived by the promise of high wages and good working conditions, the Negro workers are brought into these countries in the most horrible conditions. In a word, they are transported in the same way as chattel slaves of former days. On the plantations they are subjected to most cruel exploitation, and are prohibited from having anything to do with the native working-class population. They are looked upon as cattle and are treated accordingly.

However, the national bourgeoisie and Yankee imperialists do not limit themselves to these criminal actions. They consciously foster the feeling of national chauvinism and race prejudice among the native Negro and white workers against the Negroes from Haiti and Jamaica. Cases are not rare when these foreign black slaves become the victims of most brutal chauvinistic persecution on the part of the native workers themselves, who are made to believe that by doing so they are defending their own economic interests.

With respect to wages, both the native and foreign Negroes always receive less wages for the same amount of work as the white workers, while the imported blacks get even less than the native Negroes. Through this method of wage discrimination the imperialists and the native capitalists are able to split up the class interest of the workers into different parts and play one off against the other.

The vast majority of Negro workers in Latin America are plant-ation labourers. This is especially so in Brazil, the Central American republics, Cuba and Colombia. Thousands of them, especially West Indians, are also employed in the oil industry in Maracaribo, Venezuela.

Since the world capitalist crisis which has greatly affected the agrarian industries—banana, coffee, cocoa, rubber—as well as oil, there is great unemployment among the workers throughout

Latin America. This has had special effects upon the black workers, who are always discharged before the whites.

In Venezuela the Gomez dictatorship, supported by the social-fascist labour agents of the United States, has prohibited immigration from the West Indies. Workers who leave the country to try to secure work elsewhere will not be permitted to return.

The situation in the banana industry in Colombia and Honduras is most deplorable, Thousands of black workers are simply starving in these countries, where the banana industry has been ruined by the world crisis of capitalism.

The same state of affairs exist in Brazil, where thousands of Negro workers on the coffee plantations are now out of work. The coffee crisis has been a tremendous blow to the Negroes, who formed about 75 per cent. of the labour on these plantations. Although they were formerly forced to work under semi-feudal conditions—with little or no pay, and limited supplies of rotten food—the situation is now a thousand times worse.

In most cases they are now being driven away from the estates without money, food, clothes or shelter. Thousands of them drift into the towns, adding to the great urban unemployment, which has increased to tremendous proportions since the uprising in 1930.

The general situation in Latin America demands the closest attention, especially the Negro question, which is becoming more and more complicated, due to the causes which we have indicated above—especially the importation of foreign blacks to compete against the native labourers.

CHAPTER III

EXCLUSIVE of the millions of Negroes who live under the direct yoke of imperialism in the United States, as well as the African and West Indian colonies, there are over 15 millions who inhabit territories that are considered independent states. For example, Haiti and San Domingo in the West Indies ; Liberia and Abyssinia in Africa. However, when we examine the economical and political conditions of those countries we see that they either are, or are fast becoming, financial colonies of Yankee imperialism. For instance, Haiti, Liberia and San Domingo are already completely under the domination of American finance-capital, while Abyssinia is rapidly being drawn into the orbit of Wall Street dictatorship.

The conditions of the black toilers, workers and peasants in these countries are equally as intolerable as those we have already described in the colonies of imperialism. This is especially so in Liberia, where the toiling masses are exploited not only by foreign capitalists, but the native bourgeoisie, known as Americo-Liberians, have reduced the indigenous population to the status of chattel slaves in their own interests as well as of American imperialists (Firestone Company).

I.—HAITI

For over 15 years Haiti has been under the political domination of the United States, which maintains a military dictatorship over the island. During these years several revolts against American imperialism have broken out among the Haitian workers and peasants, but these have all been ruthlessly suppressed. It has been estimated that over 3,000 Haitians have been murdered by the United States' marines during their occupation of the country.

Because of the position of Haiti proper, which overlooks the Panama Canal and the proposed canal through Nicaragua, the island is considered the most valuable strategic base for the United States navy in the Caribbean, as well as a fertile field for the investment of finance-capital in the development of tropical products, such as coffee, cotton, tobacco, cocoa, sugar, etc., etc.

These are the principal factors which dictated the military annexation of the island in 1915.

On the occasion when the first batch of American marines landed their leader, *Admiral Caperton,* was instructed by the United

States State Department to impose a treaty with the following conditions upon the Haitians :

1. That the mining, commercial and agricultural resources of the country be developed exclusively by American financial interests.
2. That the United States was to provide a general receiver and financial adviser to the Government and thereby assume complete control over revenue.
3. That Haiti would not float any new loans or change her tariff unless first approved by the United States.
4. That Haiti would neither lease nor cede territory to any foreign power.
5. That the United States should supply officers for the Haitian gendarmerie (police force).

Since the American occupation the conditions of the 2,500,000 Haitians, especially the workers and peasants, have become terrible.

1. *Land Robbery*

Nearly all the fertile lands held by the peasants since the establishment of the republic in 1804 have been appropriated by the imperialists and turned into large plantations controlled by foreign corporations. As a result of this policy most of the Haitians are now a landless proletariat and are compelled to become wage-earners on the plantations and in the factories of foreign corporations.

So intense has been the policy of exploitation and its effects upon the living standards of the toiling masses, that spontaneous revolts have broken out throughout the island from time to time. All these manifestations of the workers for liberation have been ruthlessly stamped out. The marines have spread a network of terrorism throughout the country. They have muzzled the press, abolished freedom of speech and assembly, and either exiled or thrown into prison all who dared to champion the cause of national independence.

In order effectively to carry out this programme of subjugation the United States State Department maintains naval rule under the direct supervision of a High Commissioner, *General John H. Russell*. This marine officer is the real dictator of Haiti. He operates through a puppet president, *Louis Bruneo*, and a *Council of State*. This council is a small committee or cabinet selected by the "president" from among his henchmen, who in turn select the "president." Both the council and the "presidents" must be approved of by the High Commission, who in turn is responsible to the United States Government in *Washington*. Thus the Haitians have absolutely no voice in the Government.

All of the large plantations, railroads, street railways, electric

E

and gas companies in Haiti are owned by American bankers. Thousands of natives are employed as unskilled labourers in these concerns. The average wage of a Haitian worker is between 20 and 30 cents a day. Wherever they are employed, whether on the plantations or in the factories, they are forced to work long hours, and are most brutally treated by the American superintendents and managers, who are some of the most cruel slave-drivers to be found in the colonies.

The *Tipinor* and the *Reginier-Pinerd Companies,* which own some of the largest coffee plantations in the island, have the reputation of being the most brutal exploiters. They employ over 10,000 Negroes, who are supposed to get one dollar a day ; but out of this a tax of 75 cents is collected and turned over to the Government, in order to meet its interest on foreign loans. The balance goes to the workers, who are expected to provide themselves with food, clothing and shelter during the period of their contract.

Exclusive of the agricultural and transport workers, there are about 5,000 stevedores employed by European and American steamship companies at Port-au-Prince, the national capital. The rate of wage is between 40 and 50 cents for loading and unloading ships. These workers are unorganised, and as a result their labour-power is being exploited to the maximum. The stevedores, together with the railroad and factory workers in the sugar refineries, form the bulk of the industrial proletariat of Haiti.

Thousands of women and children are also employed as agricultural labourers on the coffee and tobacco plantations. These workers are even more viciously exploited than the men. The average wage for women is 15 cents per day and children 10 cents. Like the men, women and children work from 10 to 15 hours under the most awful conditions, especially during the rainy season of the year, when malaria is very prevalent. The low standard of living among the Haitian toilers due to small wages and the rationalisation of the American capitalists contribute to the high mortality. The majority of Haitian agricultural workers suffer from hookworm and other tropical diseases.

2. Black Ivory Trade

Faced with starvation at home, tens of thousands of Haitian peasants emigrate to the various neighbouring colonies. Most of these labourers, induced by promises of high wages, go to Cuba under agreement with American sugar companies for the purpose of cutting sugar canes. In the past these annual migrations have had the effect of relieving unemployment in Haiti, but during the last year or two emigration has dropped off considerably as a result of the sugar crisis in Cuba. This country can no longer absorb the surplus labour of Haiti. During the years of migration the Haitian Government, by imposing a head tax on those leaving the country, was able to raise thousands of dollars annually.

The migration of blacks to the Spanish speaking islands has created a new problem for the Caribbean labour movement. Formerly there was no coloured problem in the West Indies such as exists in the United States and South Africa. The black Haitians for the most part were confined to their country, while the Spanish speaking whites and mulattoes lived in Cuba and Porto-Rico. But during the years of the development of the sugar industry in Cuba the American imperialists have been able to use the Haitians against the Spanish speaking workers in order to worsen the economic conditions of the Cubans. This has created much racial feeling between the two groups.

This "Black Ivory" trade flourished under the special decree promulgated during the presidency of General Jose Miguel Gomez. In order to stimulate the trade the General Sugar Company, the largest American concern in Cuba, used to pay 25 dollars for every Haitian delivered on its reservations. During the boom years of the sugar industry trading in Negroes became so profitable that steamship companies operating between Haiti and Cuba made fortunes in the transportation of these black slaves.

Once in Cuba the Haitians are left surrounded by armed guards to the sugar plantations and housed there in large wooden barracks, in which many couples live and sleep without any partitions between them, and without any sanitary provisions except a hole in the ground at the end of the structure they occupy as living quarters.

As they cannot get out of the enclosure during the entire time of the "contract," they must buy all provisions in the company store and usually, at the end of the crop, are indebted to the contractors. Some remain on the plantations over the "dead" season and shift for themselves as best they can. The plantation owners, however, are often "kind" enough to allow them to remain in the barracks without exacting rent from them during the off season, thus saving the expense of paying to transport new slaves during the succeeding crop season. In the enclosure, the Negroes are "protected" by armed company guards, equipped with rifle and machine guns as well as rubber whips. These guards are never reluctant to shoot at anyone attempting to escape.

The Haitians are paid less than 25 cents per day during the five months of crop gathering. Whenever they protest or revolt against bad treatment the unrest is always settled by the guns of the guards.

It has been estimated that over 40,000 Haitians were imported into Cuba in 1920. This number, however, dropped to 5,000 in 1922, due to the sugar crisis in that year. The number again rose to 14,312 in 1927, but since then the number has been on a steady decline. This slave trade is now being directed from

Cuba to the Latin American mainland. For example, during the banana strike in Colombia in 1928 the United Fruit Company, an American corporation, imported thousands of Haitians and Jamaicans in order to break the strike of the Colombian workers. Since then the company has applied to the Colombian Government for permission to import 10,000 Negroes from the islands. This request will certainly be granted, as Columbia is one of the vassal states of Yankee imperialism.

The present policy of the American capitalists in the Caribbees and Latin America is to create and foster artificial racial differences among the toiling masses, and by so doing divide the workers and thereby exploit all of them more effectively.

These high-handed methods of imperialist exploitation, perpetrated against the Haitians, especially the peasantry, were the underlying factors which led to the revolt in November, 1928, which was drowned in blood by the machine guns of the United States marines.

II.—LIBERIA

This republic, like Haiti, is a typical colonial country. It is situated on the west coast of Africa between the British colony of Sierra Leone and the French colony of Ivory Coast. The country covers an area of 43,000 square miles, with a coast line of 350 miles. The population is about 2,500,000. Of this number 20,000 are " Americo-Liberians," Negroes whose ancestors were once slaves in America, but returned and settled in the country during the early days of its colonisation. There are also 500 Negro British subjects, and 400 Europeans and white Americans. The great bulk of the population consists of various indigenous peoples.

1. *Firestone Dictatorship*

After the great war America found herself confronted with the necessity of competing against the British rubber monopoly. As rubber is an indispensable product in the automobile industry of the United States, a conference was called by the rubber manufacturers in which the United States Government participated. At this conference it was agreed that the United States Government would actively co-operate with the industrialists in producing a tropical sphere of interest in order that they might produce their own rubber. This plan created an outlet for the capitalists to invest more finance-capital in Africa. President Hoover, the then Secretary of Commerce, was the official spokesman of the Government in this imperialistic project.

In July, 1925, the Firestone Rubber Corporation, one of the biggest rubber trusts in the world, entered into negotiations with the Liberian Government for a lease on rubber producing lands. The company secured the concession of a million acres of land at the cost of six cents per acre.

After the negotiations were completed the Firestone Company demanded that the Liberian Government accept a loan of $5,000,000 at the rate of 7 per cent. interest, failing which they (Firestone) would not carry through the proposed development scheme.   The Liberian people were reluctant to accept this heavy financial obligation, but finally succumbed to the coercion of the great colossus of the North.

One of the greatest obstacles which have stood in the way of the economic development of the republic has been the lack of transportation.   In this respect Liberia is mediæval when compared with the British and French colonies on the west coast of Africa. There are no railroads in the country, while roads suitable for vehicular traffic only exist in the principal towns.   The only means of communication between the hinterland and the seaports is on animal back over mud-covered forest tracks and bridgeless rivers. This is the reason why the Firestone Company was so insistent upon the Government accepting the loan in order that funds might be provided for the construction of railways and motor roads, as well as the improvement of the harbour of Monrovia.   The terms of the loan therefore especially stipulate that half of the money has to be expended on public works, while the other half is to be used in payment of certain outstanding public debts.   The proposed road-building scheme will greatly facilitate the company's transport of its raw produce from the plantation.

2. *Slavery Unearthed*

In order to carry through the imperialist project of large-scale plantations, the Firestone Corporation has been confronted with two major problems : (1) CONFISCATION OF NATIVE LANDS, and (2) AN ADEQUATE SUPPLY OF CHEAP LABOUR.   The Liberian Government, headed by President King, has actively co-operated in both respects.

The majority of indigenous population still inhabit the interior of the republic.   Although they nominally acknowledge the authority of the Central Government in Monrovia, they nevertheless retain their own forms of tribal, social and political institutions. Now that the Liberian legislature has expropriated their lands and given them away to the Firestone Company, the natives are resisting the attempts of the rubber interests to turn them into wage slaves.   This has already led to several uprisings, which have been put down by the Liberian military force.

By enlisting the services of various Americo-Liberian officials, such as administrators of provinces and districts, as well as native chiefs, the American imperialists are gradually succeeding in getting the peasants to leave their villages and work on the rubber plantations.   Over 40,000 men have already been recruited and turned over to the Firestone Concession.   This recruiting is carried out largely under the orders of the chiefs, who are paid one cent for every worker supplied. The Government has also established a central Labour Bureau with branches in various parts of the country, through which able-bodied Negroes are conscripted into labour battalions and shipped off to the plantations. The Government also receives a commission for each man supplied. The workers get about three cents a day, and are compelled to labour 14 and 15 hours under the most brutal and demoralising conditions.

In some parts of the Republic actual slavery exists. Kathleen Simon, the wife of the British Liberal, Sir John Simon, in her book entitled " Slavery," states : " Whether the number of slaves in Liberia is 100,000 or 500,000 no one can say. Equally it is difficult for anyone to deny that slave-owning and slave-trading prevail over wide areas of the country." Open charges against the Liberian Government for promoting the slave-trade have been made by Dr. Buell in America, and Mr. John H. Harris of England, before the League of Nations, and more recently by Mr. Roland Faulkner, a Liberian Senator.

Mr. W. G. Gibson, the Liberian Secretary of State, in a letter in reply to the allegation of Faulkner, published in the " Liberian Times," admitted that thousands of natives are recruited in the interior and brought to the ports of the country and shipped to the Spanish Islands of Fernando Po and other African colonies. Mr. Gibson said : " All of us (Liberian officials) know that it is a transaction authorised by law and sealed by contract and agreement. Whether we agree with the law or not is another question."

This statement shows that the Government not only knows of the existence of slavery, but actually legalised the system in order to enable a few degenerate black politicians to enjoy a parasitic existence by turning over thousands of native toilers to the Portuguese slave dealers.

The slave trade of Liberia has become such an international scandal that even the League of Nations has been forced to make a gesture.

An international commission composed of the following representatives was appointed last April to investigate the charges : Dr. Cuthbrust Christ, on behalf of the League of Nations Secretariat, Dr. Charles S. Johnstone, a well-known Negro Sociologist and Professor of Fisk University, on behalf of the United States, and the Hon. Arthur Barclay, a former Liberian.

The Commission, despite its attempts to whitewash the Government, was compelled to admit that inter and intra-tribe domestic slavery existed. The Commission also stated that the pawning of human beings was widespread throughout the country. Forced labour has also been widely used, both by the Government and by private persons, chiefly for road-making, erecting public buildings and porterage. This system has also been largely abused by many officials of the Government, as well as soldiers, who use these slaves to cultivate their own farms. With respect to the exportation of labour the Commission discovered that large contingents of labourers were recruited from the indigenous populations and shipped to Fernando Po and French Gaboon on conditions scarcely distinguishable from the old methods of slave trading and slave raiding.

As was to be expected, the commissioners entirely exonerated the American imperialists for the part they played in recruiting forced labour, by stating in their report that they " discovered no evidence that Firestone Co. ' consciously ' employed forced labour." This is nonsense ! The commissioners know better. They found no evidence against Firestone because they knew that if they did it would be more embarrassing for the United States Government to take official action.

Such a statement that the Company did not " consciously " employ forced labour is merely a shrewd way of whitewashing Firestone and its agents, and at the same time providing the United States Government with the pretext for assuming still greater political control over the republic in the form of a protectorate.

This will no doubt justify the fears expressed by the British imperialists in their organ, " The African World," of October 5th, 1929, which, commenting editorially on the Liberian situation, stated :

" No one who follows the question would be surprised if, as the outcome of the Commission, the United States were invited to take the more definite administrative interests in Liberia. It is thought that America may be prepared to enter upon an extension of a colonial policy in West Africa."

It has been announced that the Firestone Company has established a bank in Monrovia as the official bank of the country.

We can, therefore, see definite indications of a movement in this direction.

3. Labour and the Crisis

Exclusive of the plantation labourers who represent the forced labour class in Liberia there are a few wage workers such as carpenters, masons, mechanics, shipwrights, etc., in Monrovia. At various ports along the coast hundreds of men and boys belonging to the Kroc tribe are employed as stevedores, boatmen and sailors by European and American steamship companies operating in West Africa. The average wage of these marine workers is 20 to 24 cents per day of 12 hours.

The following incident gives us an idea of the condition under which these black seamen are forced to work. " In 1924 fourteen Kroc boys complained that they had been unjustly imprisoned in Warri, a port in Nigeria, as a result of the complaint of a British captain, their employer, who charged that they had refused to obey his orders. The boys stated that they had been frequently compelled to work overtime from three o'clock in the morning to mid-night—twenty-one of twenty-four hours; and that at Warri they had worked storing palm-oil from three o'clock one morning to one o'clock the following morning, when they were given permission to rest. At 2.45 a.m. they were ordered to scrub down the deck. At the same time the captain upbraided them for having left three casks of oil on deck. The boys by this time ' began to jeer and to behave insolently,' whereupon the captain had them arrested and they were placed in a British prison while the steamer sailed away." (Buell: " Native Problem in Africa " Vol. ii, Page 775). From time to time spontaneous strikes break out on board ships, but these are invariably nipped in the bud largely because of the lack of organisation and leadership.

During the year 1930 the already low standard of living of these workers has fallen even lower, due to the acute economic and financial crisis in the republic, for Liberia, like all colonial countries, is in the grip of the agrarian crisis.

III.—SAN DOMINGO

San Domingo is one of the two Negro republics in the West Indies. Geographically it forms part of the island of Haiti, to which it was politically subordinated until 1844. The republic occupies the eastern portion of the island, and is estimated to be over 19,000 square miles with a population of 800,000. San Domingo has a rather cosmopolitan population. But the vast majority of the people are Negroid. Unlike Haiti, which largely reflects French civilisation, the people of San Domingo are Spanish in language and culture. San Domingo was the first country in the Caribbean to be brought under the domination of American imperialism, which established a military dictatorship over the republic. Since 1914 the finances of the country have been under the control of American bankers. The first foreign loan made to San Domingo by the National City Bank was to the extent of $1,400,000. This was followed by another loan of $20,000 by the banking firm of Kuhn, Loeb & Co., in return for which the Customs administration of the country was placed in the hands of American officials. The financial obligations soon involved San Domingo in political difficulties with the United States. Taking advantage of the situation, the Yankee imperialists landed more soldiers in the country to strengthen their stranglehold over the republic. The policy which followed in the wake of this intervention was one of bloodshed and terror. According to evidence given at the hearings before a United States Commission, " The Government treasury was seized; the national congress was dismissed; elections were prohibited; thousands of marines were spread over the country and with unlimited authority over the natives; public meetings were not permitted; . . . destructive bombs were dropped from airplanes upon towns and hamlets; every home was searched for arms, weapons, and implements ; homes were burned ; natives were killed ; tortures and cruelities committed ; and 'Butcher' Weyler's horrible concentration camps were established. . . . Repressions and oppressions followed in succession.   When protests were made the protestants were fined heavily and also imprisoned, and when resistance or defence was attempted, bullets and bayonets were used.   Criticism of the acts of the military government were not permitted . . . and those who violated the order were severely punished by fines and imprisonment. . . . The Dominican people have been 'taxed without representation' and the money so raised expended recklessly and without in any way consulting them. . . . For five years this policy of suppression, repression, oppression and maladministration has continued."

As was to be expected, the toiling population of San Domingo were the greatest sufferers.   Before the intervention San Domingo was a country of peasant proprietors.   But after the American bankers abrogated the constitution which safeguarded the peasants' economic rights and confiscated the land, which was turned into large plantations for the cultivation of sugar, coffee, cotton and other tropical products.   The peasants, having been driven off the land, are forced to pay exorbitant taxes and to become the wage slaves of the Yankee landlords.   With small wages, long hours, filthy and insanitary living conditions in the plantation barracks, the death rate among the San Dominican population has increased to astonishing proportions within recent years.

The natives have revolted from time to time.   These uprisings have greatly affected the stability of the country, resulting in financial losses to the foreign capitalists.   As a result of this the United States Government has been forced to withdraw its marines. But the mailed fist of Wall Street still continues to dominate the economic and political life of the country.   In order to maintain its policy of subjecting and enslaving the toiling masses the American bankers have from time to time supported various native puppet presidents through whom they carried out their imperialist design. These colonial lackeys have been just as ruthless as their imperialist masters.   The last administration, headed by President Velasquez, was of such a notorious fascist character that even the petty-bourgeoisie, whose economic interests have been rigidly subordinated to the interest of foreign finance-capital, revolted, and, with the aid of the agrarian masses, overthrew the Velasquez regime in 1930.

This petty-bourgeois *coup d'état* has not relieved the misery of the workers of San Domingo.   On account of the agrarian crisis, which has greatly affected the economic life of the country, absolutely dependent upon agriculture, widespread misery has seized the country.   This has given rise to a tremendous wave of strikes among the agricultural workers and general unrest throughout the entire country.   The imperialists who control the sugar industry are trying to find a solution for the crisis by launching a most violent offensive against the workers. The vast sugar plantations are cutting expenses to the bone. Even weeding, the cheapest class of labour, is not being undertaken. And, where this work is absolutely necessary, it is being done by contract, so that the fastest workers can hardly earn 20 cents per day. Although native food is plentiful and cheap, due to the falling off in export trade (for example, fish could be purchased as low as 3 cents a pound, and 5 cents' worth of sweet potatoes would feed an average family for several days), very few workers can earn as much as 8 cents a week in San Domingo to-day, as a result of which thousands of natives are gradually dying from starvation.

Added to this economic depression greater misery has been caused by the devastating hurricanes which swept over San Domingo during September, 1930. The entire rural districts of San Domingo were laid waste. Hundreds of men, women and children who were without food and clothing invaded the capital and broke into the shops and warehouses. Only the intervention of the Dominican army and United States marines prevented another revolution. In order to appease the starving population the Government has been forced to grant relief to the starving masses. The inadequacy of this, however, led to several clashes between the civilian population and the military. One of the biggest strikes occurred in central *La Rumana*, in the southern portion of the country, where hundreds of West Indian Negroes have been evicted from the barracks which they occupied on sugar cane plantations. The *La Rumana* plantations are owned by the American controlled South Porto Rican Company and cover an area of 40 square miles, and like all foreign agricultural interests in San Domingo are administered as a sort of independent principality. For instance, the *La Rumana* Company controls its own railroad, police and other administrative machinery, under the supervision of American officials. One of the difficulties which the sugar companies have always experienced is in obtaining an adequate supply of labour. Native Dominicans will not work in the fields for less than $1.25 per day; Negroes are brought from neighbouring West Indian islands, especially Jamaica, to do the work and thereby reduce the standard of living of the black San Dominicans. Each imported labourer is put on a bond of $40 as a security for leaving the country at the end of the harvest season. The American companies pay the Dominican Government $3 per head for each indentured labourer. This conspiracy between the foreign capitalists and the native politicans has largely created the low standard of living forced upon the native and foreign workers. Theirs is a conscious policy of " divide and rule."

When the harvest season is over the imported natives are rounded up by the police, chained together, and marched to the shipping depots, where they are embarked like cattle on ships and sent back to their respective countries. Those who are fortunate enough to have a few dollars manage to make their escape by bribing the guards. They wander about the country seeking odd jobs until they are arrested by the police.

The misery of the toiling population of San Domingo has been described by observers as the worst that has ever been experienced in the history of the country. Over 80 per cent. of available labour is unemployed. It is not unlikely that another revolution, headed this time by the workers, will again break out in San Domingo as a result of the present intolerable conditions.

IV.—ABYSSINIA

Unlike Haiti and Liberia, Abyssinia is a feudal monarchy. Historically, it is one of the oldest kingdoms in the world, its rulers tracing their ancesters to Solomon and the Queen of Sheba, from whose descendant, Menelik, one of the greatest rulers of the country, the present monarch, Ras Tafari, claims descent.

Abyssinia covers an area of about 350,000 square miles and is situated in the north-eastern part of Africa. The population is estimated at about 10 millions, mostly blacks of Negro stock added with much Semitic blood. The economic character of the country is chiefly agricultural, based upon a feudal system. A religious hierarchy of the Coptic church plays a dominant rôle in the political life of the kingdom. The church owns about a third of all the land. The remainder is under the sovereignty of the emperor, at whose will powerful chieftains enjoy the right to cultivate the lands. Abyssinia, like Tibet, Mongolia, Afghanistan, etc., has been for centuries isolated from the western world, which accounts for its industrial and cultural backwardness. There are no industries in the country, which is entirely dependent upon pre-capitalist production. Outside the priesthood and the higher officials very few Abyssinians can read and write. Because of the dominant rôle which the church plays as the bulwark of feudalism, every attempt by the young generation of Abyssinians to break the stranglehold which the church wields, in modernising the country by means of industrialisation, meets with tremendous opposition. However, within recent years, Abyssinia has begun to be drawn into the orbit of American imperialism. In 1930 an American engineering company, the *J. G. White Engineering Corporation of New York City*, completed negotiations and secured a contract for the building of a dam on the Blue Nile, which has its source in Abyssinia. The project will cost about 25 million dollars. For years American capitalists met with much opposition from the British imperialists, who are afraid, that, if Americans are per-mitted to construct the dam, it will place them in a position to control the waters of the Nile upon which the British cotton growers in the Sudan depend. In this struggle between British and

American imperialism for the subjugation of Abyssinia the United States, by securing this concession, will soon be in a position to more firmly entrench herself in control over the economical and political affairs of the kingdom. At present Abyssinia has a special mission in the United States soliciting the co-operation of the U.S. State Department in sending technical advisers to Africa. Medical, sanitary and financial advisers have already been despatched to Abyssinia.

Ras Tafari, the new emperor, is said to be more sympathically inclined to American capitalists, who are in a better financial position than the British to undertake the industrialisation of the country. Furthermore, Great Britain, France and Italy are the three historic enemies of Abyssinia, having entered into secret treaties for the conquest and dividing up of the country. Thanks to the complete victory of the Abyssinian troops under Menelik over Italian imperialism in 1896, Abyssinia has been able to maintain her sovereignty. One of the greatest obstacles in the development of the country is the existence of domestic slavery, which is widespread.

As a result of this the toiling masses of the country are exploited in the worst way by a feudal oligarchy which holds sway of life and death over these chattel slaves.

The church is the greatest factor in the way of social emancipation. All ecclesiastical lands are cultivated by slaves in the most primitive manner. The clergy are therefore afraid that with the introduction of modern methods of agriculture, coupled with the industrialisation of the country, a free labour market will be created and the masses now held in bondage will break away from their hold.

Despite these obstacles the new regime in Abyssinia seems determined to carry through reforms. But the way in which this is being undertaken will undoubtedly play into the hands of the European and American imperialists, who are feverishly manœuvring for an opportunity to annex this country in order to better exploit its rich natural resources. The American imperialist agent, James Braun, in his book, "Savage Abyssinia," sounds the tocsin, when he says : " I had talked the subject over with several persons in Addis Ababa, who have the good of the country at heart, and was prepared to offer a suggestion : ' Why don't you invite foreign capital to come to your country, offering thirty to fifty year leases upon tracts of land for the growing of coffee, the raising of cattle, mules, horses, and for mining ? You could guarantee foreign concessions, large amounts of slave labour and make an arrangement whereby the big slave-owners—some of the Rasses own as many as 15,000 slaves—could lease their slaves to work upon such concessions at a fair wage. One half could be given to the slave-owner and the other half retained in a Government fund to purchase the slaves' freedom.' "

It is stated that the new Emperor is strongly in favour of Braun's suggestion, which is just what Wall Street wants. Events will prove ere long that the Abyssinian masses will change their present status of chattel slaves for that of wage slavery under the iron heels of foreign capitalists. The only way in which the slaves can hope to free themselves is by first striking a death-blow to the reactionary religious hierarchy and the feudal system.

PART II

CHAPTER IV

THE AWAKENING OF NEGRO TOILERS

Now that we have described some of the conditions under which Negro toilers live in various parts of the world, all of which glaringly expose the brutal and inhuman policies adopted by the various capitalist exploiters in order to extract super-profits out of the labour of these toilers, we shall now attempt briefly to chronicle some of the recent *Revolts, Uprisings* and *Strikes*, which have occurred in the different sections of the *Black World*. These counter-offensives against the imperialists are of great significance, for they demonstrate the tremendous revolutionary potentialities of the Negro toiling masses, and show their readiness to wage a relentless struggle against European and American imperialism as well as their own native and racial oppressors who are the agents and lackeys of the white imperialists.

1. SOUTH AFRICA

In this terrible land of Anglo-Boer imperialism the struggles between the natives and the capitalist oppressors are daily becoming more and more acute. Within recent years several armed clashes have occurred between the black workers and their class-conscious white allies, under the leadership of the Communist Party, against the employers and the armed forces of the South African Fascist Government.

The bourgeoisie, fearing the growing unrest of the natives, thanks to the activities of the South African Communist Party and the Non-European Federation of Trade Unions affiliated to the R.I.L.U., the only real champions for a *Black South African Republic*, conducted a series of " czarist " raids upon the native quarters in Durban in 1929. Special squads of police and soldiers were transported from Johannesburg to carry out these offensives. These armed forces were augmented by special fascist bands of hooligans.

Added to the general oppressive laws of the South African ruling class, the Government attempted to prevent the natives from brewing their own beer in order to force them to maintain the municipal beer houses. This the natives refused to do and organised a general boycott on the Government shops. The women took an active part in this campaign, because they were directly affected. Due to the scandalously small wages paid the men, the women and girls are forced to manufacture and sell native beer in order to get money to help augment the family budget and pay their own taxes. This boycott was also a reflection of some of the more basic grievances under which the natives suffer. The Durban campaign soon spread throughout the country, arousing thousands of workers to active demonstration against taxation and the Pass laws. Everywhere the Government tax-gatherers met with active resistance. The bloody Hertzog Government, taking advantage of this as a pretext, declared open war on the blacks. The military department, together with the Minister of Justice, *Oswald Pirow*, mobilised squads of military and armed police and despatched them to all the centres where the natives had defied the State. *Durban* was the centre of the most vicious onslaught. Early one morning, while the entire native quarter was asleep, soldiers broke into their shacks and without the slightest warning began to shoot and bayonet men, women and children. Machine guns and tear gas were also freely used in this raid. Again British imperialism had triumphed! The only difference was that MacDonald's " Labour " and not the Conservative Government was in office. True to their social-imperialist rôle these arch-hypocrites, who glibly talk about *Pax Britannica*, had no word of protest and condemnation to offer to Hertzog and his gang of murderers. But the blood of these African martyrs was not shed in vain. The natives, instead of becoming cowed and intimidated, began to organise their forces under the leadership of the Communist Party and to wage a counter-offensive against their fascist oppressors. Although without arms (South African capitalists will not sell Negroes guns nor does the law permit them to bear arms), they took possession of the streets not only in Durban, but in other cities, especially *Potchefstroom* in the Transvaal, where demonstrations and meetings were held as protests against the Hertzog Government.

At some of these meetings the natives not only pledged themselves to carry on the fight against white terror, but burned the effigies of *Pirow*, *Hertzog*, *Smuts* and other representatives of the bourgeoisie. During one of the demonstrations held in Cape Town the authorities attempted to prohibit a procession of the natives. The workers became more defiant, ignored the police orders and refused to give up possession of the streets. A few days later a clash occurred between the natives and the fascists at Potchefstroom, where four natives and a number of Europeans were wounded.

The demonstrations against fascism reached a climax on *Dingaan's Day* in 1929, the occasion on which the South African bourgeoisie celebrated the anniversary of their " victory " over the Zulus led by chief Dingaan. In former years this was an exclusive imperialist holiday, but in 1928 the natives for the first time staged a counterdemonstration against their overlords. Thousands of natives participated. The fascists made an attack upon the black workers which developed into a free fight, during which a Negro worker, one of the most outstanding revolutionary fighters, was shot. On the occasion of his funeral the natives, disregarding the attempts of the police to break up their procession, marched through the main centres of Durban with banners bearing revolutionary slogans. The procession stopped at intervals to renew their pledges of carrying on the fight in revenge for the cowardly death of their comrade.

The provocative actions of the Government in order to provide some pretext for spilling more native blood still continue. Almost every week the tax collectors, accompanied by a squad of armed policemen, make raids upon the native sections through the industrial centres of South Africa. The general procedure on these occasions is to concentrate the armed forces in some secret place in close proximity to the workers' tenements. The raids take place early in the mornings when the workers and their families are asleep. At a given signal by the chief tax-gatherer the police rush on the huts and with the butts of their guns break down the doors and enter. They then demand that the workers show their Poll tax receipts. Those who cannot produce their slave badges are arrested and marched off to jail. But worst of all is the treatment accorded to the native prisoners. No distinction is made between men, women and children. They are all treated alike—cuffed, kicked, flogged and handcuffed. The next stage is to take the natives before a magistrate who imposes fines upon them which they cannot pay, with the result that they are turned over to some capitalists who make them work out the amount of the fines. According to the "South African Worker," 26-9-30, one of the biggest raids took place in Johannesburg in August, 1930. Over 800 natives were rounded up and 270 pounds collected. A fortnight later another one was staged in Cape Town. On this occasion 250 natives were taken prisoners. This was followed by another in Kimberley ; approximately 1,000 workers were arrested. The most unusual thing about the Kimberley affair was the fines of ten shillings each inflicted on those who had already paid their taxes, but had left their receipts at home for fear they might get lost ! The magistrate, however, told them that they must not hide away their receipts but keep them in readiness for inspection at any moment when raids are made.

A bloody outrage was committed at Worcester, a town about 60 miles from Cape Town, in May, 1930. The conditions of the agricultural workers in this district were so terrible that the workers held general meetings at which they decided to organise. As soon as this news reached the farmers and the police, a raid was organised on the workers' quarters under the pretext that they were looking for illegal liquor stills. The natives resisted the police and drove them away with sticks and stones. The police, reinforced by armed bands of white fascists, returned and shot five workers and wounded seventeen. Twenty-three of those who succeeded in escaping were afterwards arrested and thrown into jail. The revolutionary leader, *Abe Simpi*, who organised a shock troop of natives and led the counter-offensive against the Government's troops, was hunted down by special armed bands of hooligans who discovered his whereabouts in the mountains where he had fled. After a brutal assault this revolutionary fighter was thrown into one of the filthy dungeons of South African capitalism to rot away the remainder of his life.

Just a few weeks before the Worcester massacre the Government carried out an attack by means of bombing planes, with tear gas, on the native tribes in the Northern Transvaal who had gone out on revolt against certain chiefs who were the hand-picked agents of the Government, aiding in the extortion of taxes and forced labour from the natives.

Since these events the spirit of revolution has taken hold of the toiling masses in South Africa to such an extent that every day brings news to the outside world of rapidly developing class struggles in South Africa. Thanks to the desperate condition in which South African economy finds itself, the workers are more and more compelled to fight in order to avoid actual starvation, for their standard of life is already so low that it cannot stand further wage cuts and worsening without causing a complete disintegration of the social life of the toiling population.

One of the most recent manifestations of the attitude of the proletariat was during the strike on the Carnavon–East London Railroad. The workers went out on strike, but due to the betrayal by the reformist native leader, Kadalie, the Government was able to achieve what the soldiers with all their machine guns and tear gas bombs had failed to do, and that was to break the strike and arrest the militant rank and file leaders. Kadalie, the black traitor—who some years before had attempted to sell the Industrial and Commercial Union, at one time the biggest native mass trade union organisation—to Amsterdam, but was defeated through the vigilance of the masses, appealed to the workers to obey the law (Masters and Servants Act) and return to work. The men refused, but with their funds in the possession of the bureaucrats, and the refusal of the white unions to help them, they were compelled to surrender after a few weeks' bitter resistance.

The bourgeoisie, realising that their days of power are more and more becoming numbered, are making desperate efforts to bolster up their slave regime. With this object in view *Pirow*, the ideological leader of the South African fascists, introduced and had enacted two amendments to the *Riotous Assemblies Act* and the *Masters and Servants Act* respectively. The amendment to the Riotous Assemblies Act gives Pirow dictatorial powers to deport

F

any person, native or non-native, from South Africa, who carried on any political agitation among the black workers. The law also enables him arbitrarily to prohibit the holding of mass meetings by the natives. It also empowers the Minister to ban any printed material circulated among the black toiling masses. In short, Pirow has now become the *Mussolini of South Africa*.

The amendment to the Masters and Servants Act, which forms the very basis upon which South African fascism is able to enslave the natives, provides that a tax of £5 be imposed upon any black worker between the age of 19 and 50 in the Transvaal and Natal, who fails to do a minimum of three months' work for a white employer every year. The Act also provides for punishment by whipping to be inflicted on any native who fails to live up to the terms of this vicious piece of legislation.

The Government intends to remove the present leper colony from Robben Island in order to make provisions for the accommodation of all revolutionary fighters and native agitators. This island has been described as the "South African Siberia." Here native agitators will be isolated from the masses, and gradually starved to death.

By means of these legal weapons, together with the thousand and one other anti-racial and labour statutes which go to make up the South African slave code, the fascists hope to be able to carry on their government in the name of *Almighty God, the King and Democracy!* But every act of Pirow, Hertzog, Smuts and Company merely increases the revolutionary mood of the masses. For example, on the day when the above-referred-to Bills (Riotous Assemblies Act, and Masters and Servants Act) were being voted upon, the natives, led by the Communists, organised demonstrations before the Parliament buildings during which a number of the members of the Government, including Pirow, were assaulted as they attempted to leave Parliament. This they succeeded in doing only after a squad of 500 soldiers who were stationed in the basement of the building had opened fire on the demonstrators, killing a few and wounding many others.

The storm continues to gather fury from day to day, for the latest events in South Africa show that Communism is gaining great influence over the broad toiling masses who are rallying to the banner of the Communists, the only revolutionary party in the country that is actively fighting for the overthrow of capitalism and the establishing of a native republic. The Communist Party has called upon the workers to make preparations for a nationwide Dingaan's Day celebration under the revolutionary slogans : All out on the streets on Dingaan's Day ! Join in the Pass-burning campaign ! Refuse to pay Poll Tax ! Down with the slave drivers' Government ! Long live the Native Republic !

The following letter by a native worker under the caption "Break those chains," recently printed in the "South African

Worker " (Umsebeuzi), shows the fighting spirit of the masses against South African imperialism :

" Fellow African workers ! You are being called upon to demonstrate on Dingaan's Day behind the fighting banners of the I.C.U., the African National Congress and the Communist Party. You must remember it has been said that freedom will not descend from heaven ; the people themselves must work for freedom. Liberty must be earned before it can be enjoyed.

" On Dingaan's Day we are going to show the rulers of this country and their tools, like Pirow, Hertzog, Thaele, Grobler and the rest, that we want our country back, whatever it may cost. We are going to scrap those filthy passes and that blood-suckers' Poll Tax, and we are not going humbly to pray to any god to do it for us. We are going to smash the Riotous Assemblies Act and we are going to oppose Pirow's Native Service Contract Bill (which proposes to fine us £5 if we do not work for a white boss and to give us lashes if we are sent to prison under the Master and Servants Act). We are not going to tolerate any more colour-discriminating laws.

" Therefore, Africans, let us be ready for Dingaan's Day. We must adopt this slogan—' Freedom or Death.' We Africans need not fear ; we are the overwhelming majority. Through the leadership of our militant African National organisations and the Communist Party we can make a powerful mobilisation of our forces and cause the blood-suckers to sit up. If we cannot demonstrate now we are not worthy to be free men who died on the battlefield. Let us go forward in the spirit of Dingaan, Makana and Moshesh [native revolutionary leaders], to free our country from white imperialism. Down with the Poll Tax and Pass laws ! To hell with the Native Service Contract Bill ! "

How did the demonstrations pass off ?

The " Manchester Guardian " of 17-12-30, quoting Reuters' correspondent in Durban, states that :

" A serious native riot broke out in Durban following a meeting of natives to commemorate Dingaan's Day, held in the centre of the town.

" The natives formed into a procession headed by one of their number bearing a red flag. The police ordered it to break up, as processions are prohibited by the by-laws. The natives responded by pelting the police and Europeans generally with stones.

" Finally, native police, heavily armed and carrying sticks and knobkerries, charged the procession. Scenes of wild confusion ensued, ending in the general flight of the natives. Seventeen natives were taken to hospital with injuries, and one was found to be dead on arrival. Several of the injured are in a serious condition.

" It is understood that one of the natives is suffering from a bullet wound, and it is learned that this was fired by a European civilian. Before the procession was formed the natives burned over 2,000 natives' passes as well as numerous hut, dog and poll-tax receipts.

"The Minister of Justice, Mr. Pirow, was burned in effigy at a meeting of natives at Pretoria yesterday. This demonstration was the result of the strong action taken by the Minister against the unrest of native labour connected with the colour bar."

News of events in other industrial centres of South Africa had not yet reached the outside world at the time of writing, but we can rest assured that the struggles of the natives against the slave laws of the South African bourgeoisie have been and will continue to be militantly conducted until the bloody regime of the Anglo-Boers is overthrown and reflected by a *Native Toilers' Government*, with safeguards for the toiling minorities of other races.

II.—EAST AFRICA

In Kenya, Uganda, Tanganyika, the British imperialists, through increased measures of taxation and land expropriation, as well as forced labour, are provoking the natives into a state of unrest so as to provide a justification to use armed force in crushing the revolutionary movement that has been developing in East Africa for a number of years. This movement, inspired by the Indian revolutionary movement, thanks to the thousands of Indians who are residents in these colonies, has developed tremendous proportions within recent years. As an indication of this, strikes are of frequent occurrence, especially among the industrial workers in Kenya. In order to conduct the revolutionary movement on an organised scale, the natives formed the East African Native Association, which led many bitter class battles against the attempt of the employers to cut wages and of the Government to increase taxes. The early successes of the organisation won widespread support among all sections of the toiling population. Thousands of industrial and agricultural workers followed its leadership. As a result of these militant struggles the employers and the Government became alarmed and declared the Association illegal. This, however, did not prevent the workers from carrying on the struggle. In order to maintain a legal existence the association changed its name to the Kikuyu Central Association. But no sooner had it come into being than a general strike was called. Thousands of workers refused to work. Plantation labourers left the farms of the European overlords. Domestic servants refused to provide food for their imperialist masters. Within a few days all the Kikuyu Province was at a standstill. Great mass meetings and demonstrations were held in all of the native villages. *Harry Thuku*, one of the most fearless fighters in East Africa, was elected as head of the strike committee of action. Harry Thuku, together with a group of young men and

women agitators, went from village to village arousing the masses
and organising them in support of the struggle. Branches of the
association were established everywhere. In Nairobi over 20,000
workers enrolled at one meeting. The method adopted by Thuku
in organising the agrarian masses was as follows. He called together the most fearless and trustworthy members of the association, especially among the youth. After instructing them as to
the tactics to be adopted in order to evade the police and other
political agents of the Government, he directed them to go into the
village and organise sub-committees of action which were given
charge to mobilise the population. In this way the movement
was able to strike roots over widespread areas. Thuku's fearless
leadership won the admiration and support of all the oppressed
peoples, especially the children, who had been forced out of school
in order to work on the farms. They created popular songs about
their young leader and the association. As the struggle continued it took on more and more of a political character, with the
result that the Governor ordered the commander of the military
forces of Kenya to mobilise the King's African Rifles, a native
regiment under British officers, in order to suppress the mass
revolt. The imperialists first attempted to do this by arresting
Thuku, but due to the tremendous mass following and the lack
of faith, even among the soldiers, who have economic and social
ties with the toiling population, they dared not adopt this method.
The Government then resorted to trickery and cunning. The
district commissions, under whom the chiefs and headmen function,
which is known as the method of Indirect Rule, were instructed
to call these native lackeys together and inform them that Thuku
was a dangerous man, that his revolt was not only directed at the
Government but that he wanted to create a republic and make
himself the president. And furthermore, if he succeeded, he
would take away the positions from the chiefs and headmen. In
order to avoid this and thereby maintain their position their duty
was to disassociate themselves from Thuku and the nationalist
movement. As was to be expected the chiefs and headmen, bribed
by promises that the Government would increase their salaries
after the uprising was suppressed, agreed to sign a proclamation
prepared by agents of the Government, in which they appealed to
the masses to return back to work under the pretext that the
Government intended to reduce taxation and to force the employers
to increase wages. Misled by these demagogic appeals, the workers
gradually began to desert Thuku and the Kikuyu organisation.
The Government, taking advantage of the situation, sent an army
of soldiers to Thuku's house and arrested him. Simultaneous with
this arrest the headquarters of the native movement at Nairobi
was raided, and all of the records and documents of the association
seized and removed to police headquarters. As soon as news of
this incident became known the members of the central com-

mittee of the association issued an appeal to the workers in which they exposed the treachery of the Government and the chiefs.   A general strike was again called, which met with as much success as the first one.   Monster mass meetings were held in the public square in Nairobi, at which a special deputation was elected and mandated to interview the Governor in order to put forward the demands of the workers, among which was the immediate release of Thuku.   The Governor was away, but his assistant informed the deputation that he was prepared to listen to their demands at a conference, but before this could take place the deputation must request the people to disperse.   The workers refused to accede to this demand.   They immediately marched to the prison where Thuku was held and insisted upon remaining there until their leader was liberated.   The Government then brought out armoured cars and machine guns on the streets.   But before the workers could disperse the officers ordered the soldiers to fire upon the crowd.   According to a letter published in " Manchester Guardian " of March 20th, 1929, by a European who had witnessed the slaughter, 150 were killed.   A very much larger number after- wards died from wounds, for relatives and friends took the wounded away and did not report these deaths for fear that they themselves would have been arrested as participants in the demonstration. Despite this massacre the workers persisted to reappear on the street.   They continued to clamour for the freedom of Thuku. The Government, realising that even with the use of armoured cars and machine guns they could not crush the revolutionary spirit of the workers, again resorted to trickery.   The officials sent out a rumour that Thuku would be removed from the prison at a certain hour.   At the appointed time they drove a car, sur- rounded by a police escort, from the direction of the prison towards another police station.   The workers, believing that their leader was really being transported in the automobile, began following it in order to fight for his release.   After the crowd had got some distance away from the prison, and before they could discover the hoax played upon them, the officials hustled Thuku into another car, drove him out of the city and lodged him in another prison about 50 miles away.   After this the Government launched a reign of terrorism.   The soldiers with fixed bayonets marched through the workers' quarters and carried out wholesale arrests.   Hundreds of such victims were given from 2 to 3 years' imprisonment.   Others were fined from 10 to 20 shillings for having been absent from .work without the permission of their masters.   When we remember that the wages of most of these workers hardly exceed a few shillings per month we can appreciate the hardship that the fines imposed upon them, for this meant months of labour without pay in order to liquidate the court fines.

All associations have since been declared illegal.   All forms of agitation and organisation among the natives of Kenya meet with the most brutal reprisals. Since the dissolution of the Kikuyu organisation the chiefs have been encouraged to form their own, which are merely pawns in the hands of the officials through which the Government is able to carry out its bloody rule.

However, despite all these attempts of British imperialism to keep the natives in a condition of slavery, the very conditions under which they live force them to find ways and means to carry on the struggle.

In November, 1929, Sir Edward Grigg, the Governor of Kenya, was compelled to admit in a dispatch to the British Colonial Office that the situation in Kenya was again assuming alarming proportions. For example, in the districts of *Lumdwa* and *Masi* the workers had denounced the chiefs as agents of the British and had driven many of them away from the villages. They also attacked the Government tax-agents. Special contingents of the King's African Rifles had to be sent into the districts where the unrest had broken out in order to disarm the natives. In order to suppress the growing anti-British movement which is taking place throughout the East African colonies, the representatives of MacDonald's " Labour " Government have ordered the chiefs to prohibit the holding of mass meetings and to report on the activities of native agitators so as to have them arrested and deported.

During the summer of 1929 the natives of Uganda attempted to organise. While holding a meeting in a chapel the British officials, accompanied by squads of armed police, made a sudden raid upon the meeting, where five natives were shot and thirty wounded. The local government, as well as the Colonial Office of MacDonald's " Socialist " Government, justified this provocative attack on the ground that strong measures were necessary to stamp out " sedition."

In Basutoland the peasants have also organised an association called the *Lakho-La-Baffo*, which is affiliated to the League Against Imperialism. This association carried on the struggle against British oppression in that country. It is made up largely of peasants whose warlike traditions have been a thorn in the flesh of the British imperialists. Revolts have frequently occurred among these tribesmen in recent years, and have only been suppressed by the use of military planes attacking the villages with bombs. Due to the isolation from the native population in South Africa on the one hand, and the military vigilance of the British on the other, the Basutos have not been able to consolidate these forces with those of the Union of South Africa, which is necessary to guarantee a successful uprising. The organisation, however, repudiates any attempt at compromise in the struggle with their oppressors, and is facing the question of armed struggle of the toiling masses as the only means of freeing themselves from British imperialism.

III.—WEST AFRICA

1. *Nigeria*

Despite the attempts of the Nigerian Government to whitewash its bloody deeds in connection with the shooting of 83 unarmed women and the wounding of 87 others in December, 1929, the general discontent and widespread unrest which has seized the country has forced the Government to publish the findings of the *Special Commission* which was appointed to investigate the causes for the uprising.

The world economic crisis of capitalism has had a tremendous effect upon Nigeria. As a result of the agrarian crisis thousands of peasants have been ruined, due to the catastrophic fall in the prices of their principal commodities, such as palm kernels, palm oil, cocoa, ground nuts and cotton. This in turn has greatly affected the finances of the country, which to a very considerable extent are derived from Custom duties on imports and exports. So the Government, in order to find a way out of its financial dilemma, attempted to throw the whole burden upon the toiling masses, especially the peasants, by increasing direct taxation upon them. The Government, however, realised that this was a delicate undertaking in the light of the pauperised condition of these overtaxed toilers, so the British political officials mobilised the chiefs in the territories assessed and instructed them to impose a special tax on the women, as the men had previously been taxed. In this way the Government hoped to force the women and children to leave the villages and seek work on the plantations and other industries owned by foreign capitalists in order to provide the money to pay the tax-gatherers. But, instead of submitting to this high-handed imperialist policy, over 30,000 women organised monster protest demonstrations against the British imperialists and their agents, the " warrant " chiefs (chiefs selected by the Government). They carried out a series of offensives against the Europeans, especially the banks and the trading companies, their principal economic exploiters. They broke into these business places and seized the buildings for days. It was only after the " Labour "–Imperialist Government of MacDonald had instructed the Governor to order troops to the scene that the uprising was crushed. This was followed by bloody reprisals. Hundreds of people were arrested and thrown into jail, scores of huts burnt to the ground and fields laid waste, all in order to intimidate the natives and subdue their militancy. For days after the revolt the areas where the fighting had occurred were converted into military camps. Martial law was proclaimed, and a rigid censorship imposed on the native press in order to prevent news from reaching the outside world. The Governor even went to the extent of calling a meeting of all the African editors in Lagos, the capital of Nigeria, at which he informed them that if they dared to print any news of what was happening in the South Eastern Province they would be subjected to imprisonment under the Public Safety Statutes of the Criminal Code.

In the face of such bureaucratic terrorism it was difficult for the world to know what was going on for several days. However, after the suppression of the uprising, the Government issued a *communiqué* in which it gave a most distorted account of the events and justified its murderous onslaught on the African women. *Dr. Drummond Shiels*, Under-Secretary of State for the Colonies, in answer to a question put to him in the House of Commons in connection with the shooting, exonerated the Nigerian Government, and even went to the extent of saying " that the Colonial Office was satisfied that the officials on the spot acted in the best interest of the country."

In keeping with the usual hypocritical gestures of British imperialism, a committee was appointed under the presidency of Major de Birell Grey, the Resident of the Colony of Lagos, and Mr. H. W. Blackall, the Government legal advisor.

After a so-called investigation into the circumstances of the uprising they issued a report which was placed before the Legislative Council and approved by the Government's majority.

This infamous document described the heroic struggle of the natives as an attempt at mob-law, and justified the firing of the troops in order to protect the property of the British capitalists.

The publication of this report merely added fuel to the fire. The natives held mass meetings in various sections of the country at which resolutions were drawn up denouncing the report. The workers also protested against taxation and other political and social disadvantages with which they are burdened. They refused to pay more taxes and threatened to renew the struggle. The Government became alarmed at this widespread discontent and appointed a second Commission. The natives threatened to boycott this commission unless they were permitted representation on it. After much reluctancy, the Government consented to include two Africans. The Commission was finally organised in February, 1930, and consisted of the following : The Hon. Donald Kingdon, Chief Justice of Nigeria, chairman ; Messrs. J. R. Osborne and Graham Paul, representing banking and commercial interests respectively ; Mr. W. Hunt, Government official, Mr. E. C. Moore and Sir Kitoyi the African representatives.

The Commission immediately began its work by visiting the disturbed areas, where witnesses were examined and a general survey carried out. On the basis of its investigation the Commission published its findings in the middle of August, 1930. The report was unanimous with the exception of one or two reservations by the European representatives of finance-capital. It gives the main contributory causes for the revolt as follows :

(1) Discontent caused by taxation of men introduced in the

affected provinces in 1928; also the widespread belief throughout the areas where the revolts took place that the Governor was about to introduce a direct tax upon women ;

(2) Discontent at the persecution, extortion and corruption practised by the chiefs and members of the native courts who were appointed by British political officers, to whom they are responsible and not to the toiling masses ; and

(3) The low price which the peasants are receiving for their raw produce and the high prices they are made to pay for imported commodities by European trading companies. With respect to the suppression of the disturbances, the report points out that large numbers of troops of the Royal West African Frontier Force were employed in addition to the armed constabulary; that firing took place thirteen times. Rifles and machine guns were used. The report finds that the fi ing was justified on most occasions.

Nevertheless, Sir Frank Baddelev, the Colonial Secretary of Nigeria, speaking at a dinner of the Colonial Conference in London, said that " the revolt was the work of the agents of Moscow. The Government had discovered the circulation of the ' Negro Worker,' a trade union journal published by the R.I.L.U. in Moscow, among the workers of Lagos, and was adopting every precaution to prevent the spreading of Bolshevism among the natives."

In concluding its report the Commission makes a number of recommendations : (1) that the system known as " lump sum assignment " should be slowly introduced with the co-operation of the chiefs and the people ; (2) that the present system of taxation should be re-examined in view of the fall in the price of produce and the widespread poverty resulting therefrom ; (3) that the Governor should appoint a special commission to inquire into the workings of the native court system, which has become the fattening house for the chiefs. The Commission also points out that the Government must pay more attention to the political influence of the women. In this respect is it very significant to note what " The Times " correspondent in Nigeria wrote :

" The trouble was of a nature and extent unprecedented in Nigeria. In a country where the women throughout the centuries have remained in subjection to the men, this was eventually a women's movement, organised, developed and carried out by the women, without either the help or commission of their menfolk, though probably with their tacit sympathy."

Yet in the face of all of these facts the Governor of Nigeria, since the publication of the report, had the audacity to impose a fine of £850 on the township of Aba, the capital of the Eastern Province and the storm centre of the revolt. In doing so the Governor stated that the *Collective Punishment Ordinance* of the colony entitled him to adopt this measure, in order to raise the money to reimburse the European merchants and bankers for the damages which they suffered. Again the toilers protested. The political officers of the province, faced with the possibility of another revolt, appealed to the Governor to withdraw the fine. Again the Government was forced to retreat. Nigeria is aflame ! Every day the crisis deepens and brings ruin to wider and wider sections of the peasantry. Unemployment is also increasing at astonishing proportions among the workers in the mining industries. The native petty-bourgeoisie is also being ruined. All of which is making for the radicalisation of broader and broader masses of the Nigerian population.

2. Gambia

A number of strikes of a political character have taken place in West Africa since the war. Thanks to the industrialisation and the extensive exploitation going on in these colonies the class struggle is assuming an acute form, by taking on more and more of an anti-imperialist character. For example, in October, 1930, a strike occurred in Gambia, in the course of which the workers were faced the necessity of defending their trade union organisation against the combined attacks of the foreign capitalists and the armed forces of the State. According to an account which appeared in the *Monthly Circular of the Labour Research Department* for January, 1930 :

" The trouble started early in October, when four to five hundred sailors—members of the Seamen's Society—engaged on the coastal steamers which are mostly owned by the combine, went on strike against heavy reduction of wages. Their case was that since 1920-21 there had been a systematic reduction of their wages. Up to 1920-21 the rates of pay had varied according to the size of the boat on which the sailor was employed, and the maximum and the minimum figures were as follows :

"70 ton craft—Captain, £18 ; mate, £6; sailor, £5; cook, £2 4s. per month.

12 ton craft—Captain, £4 ; mate, £3 12s. ; sailor, £3 ; cook, £2 4s.

Monthly rations—45 lbs. rice ; 10s. fish money ; one bag salt ; three gals. cotton seed oil.

Reduced Wages—Captains, £3 to £2 16s. per month, regardless of tonnage ; sailors, £1 12s. to £1 8s. ; cooks, 16s. ; fish money, 4s. ; crew to provide own salt and oil.

" In spite of the fact that the Seamen's Society was outside the Bathurst Trade Union, the latter took up their case and wrote to the Colonial Secretary to ask that the Government should intervene to bring about ' an amicable understanding,' suggesting that a board of arbitration should be appointed to inquire into the whole matter of wages and cost of living. In a letter to the Colonial Secretary, dated October 18th, the union secretary wrote :

" ' Captains have been forced to do the work of sailors ; captains and sailors have been victimised by dismissal and forfeiture of pay. Over and above all, the local seamen are employed only for three to four months of the year, so that the reduction complained of does not insure for them a living wage.'

" By October 26th the Seamen's Society had become incorporated with the Bathurst Trade Union ; on October 30th thirty-one union delegates interviewed the Governor, who refused to recognise the Union and said he could not arrange for arbitration until he had heard the case of the merchants.   The strike therefore dragged on for sixty-two days.

" In the meantime a struggle affecting a much larger number of the members of the Bathurst Trade Union was developing. Withdrawal notices were issued by the Union on behalf of : (1) shipwrights, carpenters and masons ; (2) motor engineers, motor drivers, steam-boat engineers, greasers, firemen and blacksmiths, on account of reductions of wages from 10s. to 4s. a day. In those trades, as with the seamen, if not more so, the vast majority are employed for some three or four months of the year ; during the remaining eight or nine months they have to subsist on what they can earn in those months. The Chamber of Commerce, representing the bulk of the employers affected, refused to come to an official understanding with the men, or to set up a court of arbitration as requested by the Union.

" In the middle of October Messrs. Palmine entered the fray, their Danish local manager having given three days' notice to all those of their employees who were members of the Bathurst Trade Union to quit the union or be dismissed.   In the weeks ending October 12th and October 19th Messrs. Palmine, Ltd., and Messrs. United Africa, Ltd., issued lockout notices to all their employees with a view to a reduction of wages.   The result of all this was that when the withdrawal notices and the lockout notices expired all the men affected by reductions of wages and non-recognition of the Union refused to return to work and by November hundreds of mechanics of all classes had laid down their tools and Bathurst was in the throes of its first general strike.

" The matters in dispute as given in the ' Gambia Outlook ' of November 9th were as follows : ' (1) recognition by the Chamber of Commerce of the Union's claims to represent the workers of Bathurst ; (2) regulation of minimum rates of pay for all trades. On the whole workers, according to the Union, are underpaid, the cost of living is rising, and altogether there is no justification for the systematic reduction of wages, which for years past has caused deep dissatisfaction in the ranks of the working classes.'

" As one of the specific conditions for calling off the strike, the Union demanded ' a guarantee that there would be no victimisation of Union members, reference being made to cases of such victimisation by various firms.'

" Negotiations are entered into between the Bathurst Trade

Union and the Chamber of Commerce, which recognised the Union's claim to represent the workers and for certain concessions on wages, but refused to fix minimum rates for the better-paid classes of skilled workers. At this stage matters were complicated by the police raid of November 14th, already referred to in last month's 'Circular' when, in the words of the 'Gambia Outlook' on November 6th, 'for the first time in history an armed raid was made on the civilian community, in which a cordon of police with truncheons took part, the other section being armed with rifles and fixed bayonets. Peaceful passengers were charged through the streets and up to date some 40 civilians have been reported wounded.'

" This police raid which has caused public indignation in Bathurst is said to have been occasioned by some stone-throwing around the car of the Hon. L. C. Ogden, area supervisor of Messrs. United Africa Co., Ltd. It is alleged that his chauffeur got into conflict with some strikers and that the trouble arose from this, but it is significant that neither Mr. Ogden nor the chauffeur were among the injured, most of whom were Africans, and are alleged to have been peaceful citizens. The Riot Act was not read and evidently there was no 'rioting.' In response to an immediate protest made by representative citizens the Governor gave an undertaking that 'an inquiry would be held at once into the methods used by the police to disperse the crowd.' A detachment of the Royal West African Force was brought into Bathurst, but was not used.

" The events of the 14th were merely an indication of the state of panic into which the Government had been thrown by the extent and solidarity of the general strike, which had already lasted 20 days, whilst the sailors' strike had lasted 60 days. On that day, therefore, the Colonial Secretary addressed an 'urgent' letter to the Union announcing that 'in view of the serious position which has arisen in the industry of the colony, His Excellency is prepared to appoint a Board to arbitrate if both parties are agreeable to this course.' The letter concludes, 'His Excellency feels sure that you will realise the urgency of the matter and the need, in the interests of the colony, to effect an immediate settlement.' It is interesting to find the Governor, on November 14th, waking up to the urgency of the situation which the Union had been urging him to consider ever since October 8th, and being so suddenly anxious to apply a method of solution advocated by the Union over a month earlier. By this time, of course, it was already too late ; the Union, having achieved its main objects by strike methods, did not feel called upon to give them up for the doubtful blessings of an arbitration board decision. Direct negotiations with the Chamber of Commerce were continued, and on November 16th a satisfactory settlement was reached. The exact terms as to wages are not yet to hand, but it is clear that the Union has won recognition, and that the workers are returning to work with an increase on last year's wages and a definite guarantee that there shall be no victimisation. The

Union, and the workers of Bathurst generally, are to be congratulated on a victory which has been won solely by solidarity and determination, and which will undoubtedly result in a great accession of strength to the Union.

"The attitude taken by the Governor of Gambia, Sir Edward Denham, during the dispute has been severely criticised by the Union officials. His refusal to submit the matter to arbitration on the ground that it was the 'private affair' of Bathurst firms, and their employees, and his tacit connivance at the importation of labour from outside the colony, notwithstanding the growing unemployment, is specially complained of. On October 31st, when the strike had just begun, the Governor issued a public notice intended to prevent picketing. This notice, after stating that attempts were being made 'to influence and bring pressure upon workers to leave their employments,' concluded : 'It is further notified that any person who, by intimidation or molestation, compels, persuades, or induces, or attempts to compel, persuade or induce any worker, who is willing to work, from doing so, is liable to be prosecuted under the Criminal Law.'

"It is also stated by the Acting Commissioner of Police that the Governor was aware of the action of the force on the 14th, and that he has given the men to know he is proud of their action. Since the settlement of the strike the Governor has further shown his hostility to the Union by causing it to be ejected from its meeting place—at the Mahommedan School. There is also trouble in the Public Works Department, owing to the Government decision to employ men on piece work on spite of the Union's refusal to allow its members to work under this system.

"The attitude of the Labour Government at home seems to be one of complete confidence in the Governor, in spite of the fact that he was appointed under a Conservative Government and has shown hostility to trade unionism. When the victimisation of trade unionists in Bathurst was first brought to Lord Passfield's notice on October 31st, he returned a very indifferent reply on November 6th to the effect that he had not received any report of the Governor of Gambia, and, even after further information had been sent in, an official of the Colonial Office stated on November 14th that Lord Passfield saw no good reason to call for a report. It is only when reports of the events on the 14th appeared in the press, and it had been stated that the matter would be raised in the House of Commons, that Lord Passfield tried to allay criticism by stating that he was receiving a report from the Governor. Both to answers to questions in the House and in answer to letters the Colonial Office had tried to minimise the whole affair, and to hide the fact that there has been a serious industrial crisis in Bathurst, from which the workers have emerged victorious.

"The trouble in Bathurst is merely another illustration of the effects upon the workers of capitalist rationalisation.   Up to 1920-21 the ground nut crop, which is practically the sole source of income for the natives of Gambia, was collected from up the rivers by native agents, and sold to a number of competing firms who were obliged to pay a reasonable price.   As the firms grew bigger they set up trading stations up the rivers, employed their own boats, and made even larger profits.   Amalgamations were entered into, the big firms such as Levers, the African and Eastern, etc., eating up the little ones, and prices to the native producers were gradually forced down.   The local merchants' pool for the crop —or 'participation' as it is called in Gambia—also prevented competition and forced the producers to accept whatever price they were offered.   In May last the United Africa Company was formed as an amalgamation of the Niger Co. (controlled by Lever Bros.) and the African and Eastern Trade Corporation ;   a final amalgamation in September last was made between the United Africa Ltd. and the Margarine Union (of which Palmine Ltd., is a subsidiary company) ;   this is of immense importance for Gambia, for it is the exclusive sphere of the Margarine Union's Combine. It gives the Combine a practically complete monopoly of the ground nut crop and invests the local merchants' pool for the crop with the force of official sanction given on behalf of the shareholders. In the opinion of the city editor of the ' Daily Mirror ' (September 3rd, 1929) the full benefits of the amalgamation will take some time to materialise, but the Combine will, in future, ' earn very big profits for its shareholders.' One of the methods of obtaining these big profits was, as foretold by the ' Gambia Outlook ' of September 28th, the exercise of rigid economy, and, as usual, this economy was first directed towards wages, hence the attack on the Bathurst Trade Union and the lockout notices of October, threats of dismissals of many workers, a hundred being already reported as being sacked in the Sierra Leone branches of the Combine.   In addition to this intensified exploitation of African wage-earners, this Combine is also grinding down the native farmers.

" In 1924-25, before the amalgamations had taken place, the native producer of ground nuts received from £9 to £10 per ton for his produce, on the basis of £15 to £16 per ton on the European market.   It is admitted that the producer is entitled to £9 to £10 per ton, a price which was reckoned to leave the capitalist an ample margin of profit.   But the situation now that the Combine has a monopoly is quite otherwise ;   to quote the ' Gambia Outlook ' for November 2nd :

" ' The only possible way in which the farmers can fight the exploitation of the Combine is by themselves combining, which is now proposed.' "

3. *Sierra Leone*

Several strikes have occurred in Sierra Leone.   The last one, which assumed large proportions, was the railway strike of 1926. For a number of years the employees, most of whom are natives, were frequently complaining to the Government, which owns and operates the railroads, about their general economic conditions. The protest of the workers met with no redress, so they decided to organise in spite of the prohibition placed on strikes by means of the *Masters and Servants Ordinance*, which makes it a criminal offence for a worker to go on strike. As a result of the agitation of the most militant men, the Sierra Leone Railwaymen's Union was formed. The *Union* drew up a list of demands which it presented to the European manager of railways. The Government replied by immediately dismissing some of the workers who took the initiative in the movement. The Union then decided to call a strike. The Government, on the other hand, realising that widespread sympathy prevailed among the toiling population for the railwaymen, immediately mobilised all the available military forces and concentrated them at various strategic points along the railroad. Shortly after the strike began the workers attempted to adopt the same tactics as those followed during the strike of 1919—that was to spread the strike to other industries as well as to propangandise the police force to raise demands (2,400 of the police had joined the 1919 strike when the Government refused to increase their wages).

This time the repressive methods of the State prevented these plans from materialising. Within six weeks the Government had recruited a sufficient number of strike-breakers to take the place of those who had downed tools. The militancy of the strikers was marvellous. Even the manager of railways had to admit that " in my twenty-two years of railway service I have seen strikes in England and elsewhere, but it was not until I came to Sierra Leone that I saw the disgraceful acts which were done by strikers, and there is no denying these incidents. When I left Boia two rails were removed in front of my train at one place, and another loosened. At another a rail was placed across the line ; the men lighting up the engine were stoned. When the first train arrived at Bo a mob, armed with sticks, attacked the tiain ; the rails were removed or loosened on curves, at steep banks and at the approach to a bridge ; telegraph poles were pulled down, wires cut and telegraph instruments interfered with, preventing telegraphic communication with the Protectorate."

The Governor, addressing a meeting of the Legislative Council, declared that the situation was more than an industrial dispute, " *It was a revolt against the State by its own servants.*"

Taking advantage of the widespread discontent engendered by the strike, and certain statements in the native press which hinted at rebellion, the Governor launched an attack on the Freetown municipality, the only form of representative institution then existing in the country. He declared that " the natives by supporting the strike had proved unworthy of the principle of elective representation." This type of imperialist reasoning needs no refutation—the toilers of Sierra Leone, thanks to the oppressive methods of the commercial and political agents of British imperialism, have no illusions of British justice. Commenting on the 1926 strike, Dr. Buell (Vol. I, p. 890) " *Native Problem in Africa*," writes : " This strike was of more far-reaching importance in that it has revealed the development of the same type of industrial problem in Africa which has tormented Europe and America for so many years. In Africa this problem is made infinitely more difficult by the fact that the employer is European and the employees are primitive people."

The most recent peasant outbreak occurred in Sierra Leone during the middle of February, 1931. This was one of the most serious rebellious which have broken out on the West Coast since the crisis. Despite the attempts of the British Government to suppress all information about the uprising, the native petty-bourgeois press of Sierra Leone openly writes: "The principal causes for the revolt were economic." Hundreds of natives led by a battalion of 50 men armed with guns invaded the Kambia District in Sierra Leone, which adjoins the neighbouring French colony of Guinea, in February. The peasants were led by *Hydara,* a Negro moslem leader, who is reported to have had tremendous influence over the natives of Kambia, thousands of whom he converted to Mohammedanism, and under the cloak of religion organised an anti-imperialist movement against the British Government. After arming his followers Hydara raised the standard of revolt by calling upon the peasants to refuse to pay their hut taxes and to drive the British officials away from the province. Hydara also demanded that all Crown lands in the Protectorate of Sierra Leone be confiscated and divided among the landless peasants in order they might be able to grow food to feed themselves in view of the fact that the palm kernel industry, their chief source of income, had completely collapsed, due to over-production.

In order to avoid starvation the peasants were turning their attention to the cultivation of food crops, such as rice, but the Government officials were opposed to this and were demanding the immediate payment of taxes. Hydara's agitation had tremendous influence throughout the Kambia province. The British Government attempted to arrest him, but the natives threatened death to all Europeans who entered their territory. The situation became so alarming that the central Government in Freetown ordered a detachment of the Royal West African Frontier Force to the scene of rebellion. The soldiers, mostly natives drawn from the other sections of Sierra Leone commanded by British officers, while attempting to embark in Kambia were fired upon by the insurgents. Skirmishes followed during the course of which several natives and soldiers were killed, including Hydara and

Captain H. J. Holmes, the English officer in command of the troops. After several days of fighting the soldiers, thanks to their overwhelming numbers and superior arms, were able to put down the revolt. After this, the most repressive campaign was launched. Hundreds of huts of natives who took part in the uprising were burned to the ground, and men and women arrested and thrown into jail or deported from the territory.

Although the revolt has been suppressed, great unrest still prevails throughout the Protectorate of Sierra Leone. Even the British Government, in its official *communiqué* issued by the Colonial Secretary of Sierra Leone, has been forced to admit that the Hydara movement has a tremendous influence over the natives of Sierra Leone and the French colony of Guinea.   Troops have taken possession of the Kambia District in order to terrorize the peasants and to suppress any new manifestations of open revolt.

4. *The Gold Coast*

With respect to the Gold Coast the economic situation is becoming very acute, thanks to the cocoa crisis and the tremendous growth of unemployment in agriculture and mining.   Spontaneous strikes and demonstrations are of frequent occurrence.

The farmers have organised an association of over 200,000 cocoa growers to oppose the monopoly of the British capitalists, especially the United Africa Company.   The farmers have refused to market their crops as a protest against the high-handed policy of robbery carried on by the foreign capitalists with the support of the Government.

The last outbreak which occurred among the industrial workers took place in September, 1930, at the Ariston Mines in the Prestea district of the Gold Coast.   From the limited news which broke through the censorship and reached the outside world the facts appear to be as follows :

The Company, in order to increase the exploitation of its labourers, attempted to introduce a quarterly system of paying wages instead of monthly.   The miners refused to agree to these terms and called a strike.   The European employers (managers, engineers, paymasters, etc.) organised an armed squad and marched through the surrounding native village where the workers were holding meetings, and without warning fired into the crowds, wounding about ten natives and killing five.   When news of this bloody onslaught reached the other villages near the mining area, hundreds of men and boys armed with sticks, knives and all kinds of primitive weapons marched to the mines and attacked the European quarters. The mines were closed down for several days in order to avoid a general wreckage.

IV.—THE CONGO TERRITORIES

1. *French Equatorial Africa*

Despite the idea prevalent among the petty-bourgeois Negroes, especially in the United States, that French imperialism pursues a more human and liberal policy towards its black colonial population than other imperialist powers, the bloody massacres which have occurred in the French Congo within recent years give the lie to this bourgeois propaganda. French imperialism, in order to carry out its ruthless policy, has been forced to utilise the services of its black petty-bourgeois colonials more than any other imperialist power. This is especially so in respect to its military policy, which bases itself to a considerable extent upon the militarisation of French Negroes, and just because of this France has been compelled to adopt a less openly hostile attitude towards her black bourgeoisie and petty-bourgeoisie than in the case of Great Britain and the United States. It is these very lackeys, dressed in the uniforms of these imperialist masters, who play the rôle of hangmen and enslavers of the toiling population of their own race.

One of the most bloody onslaughts that has ever been perpetrated in Africa occurred in 1928. Incited by the most oppressive measures of capitalist exploitation, some of which we have described in the previous chapter, the black toiling population of the Congo regions raised the banner of revolt against their French masters. This was the second time within four years that these people attempted to strike a blow for freedom. In 1924 the insurrection lasted several days, and was finally suppressed by the overwhelming military forces of the French Government. Thousands of natives were massacred. The revolt of 1928, like the previous one, was inspired by a series of causes, chief among them being the resentment of the natives at the inhuman way in which they had been treated by the overseers on the railroads now under construction, and in the mines; also the subjection of their women and children to forced labour on the plantations, compulsory military training among the youth, as well as the attempts of the Government to enforce taxation. However, unlike the insurrection of 1924, the last revolt showed more class-consciousness among the workers and was better organised. The revolt embraced a number of important districts in the French Equatorial region, and lasted for over four months, during which time the natives, despite their limited arms, inflicted a number of defeats on the French troops, capturing a large section of their infantry. Mines were blown up, bridges destroyed, and a number of buildings on the French concessions destroyed. The natives displayed tremendous bravery and military prowess which the French bourgeois press, despite its attempt to suppress information, has been forced to admit.

In order to stamp out the revolt, which was spreading from

village to village, French military reinforcements were brought from the military base in Finda. But even this overwhelming force met with great resistance, owing to the guerilla tactics adopted by the insurgents, who were also favoured by the great tropical forests which exist in those regions. After the revolt was finally suppressed the Government launched a campaign of terror, during which period more people were murdered than in actual combat. Every native suspected of having taken part in the uprising was shot. Old men and women were publicly whipped in the villages, as a warning to the younger generation never to attempt to do like their elders. This, however, did not prevent the natives from again rebelling in April, 1930. This time a white French revolutionary worker and several natives were arrested at Brazzaville, the capital of the Middle Congo, and sentenced to three years' imprisonment for attempting to organise a trade union. Learning of the sentence, several thousands of native workers went on strike and proceeded to the court for the purpose of demanding the freedom of their comrades. The police attempted to break up the demonstration, but were attacked with stones. The soldiers were then called out, and without any warning opened fire upon the demonstrators. The natives offered desperate resistance, throwing stones at the soldiers, during which encounters the Governor of the Middle Congo, who appeared on the scene, was wounded. For several days the business life of Brazzaville was at a standstill, during which time the native quarters were occupied by troops. The serious character of this revolt can be gleaned from the Brussels paper " Soir," whose Congo correspondent writes : *" The soldiers had to act especially energetically in the low Congo settlement near Brazzaville. This settlement is famed as the operative base of the native Communist elements."*

2. *French West Africa*

Strikes and other manifestations of discontent are of frequent occurrence in French West Africa, especially among the workers on the Thies-Niger Railway. The last widespread revolt in this region occurred in 1925 among the Bambarra tribe, most of whom are employed on railroad construction. The immediate cause for this revolt was the attempt of the Government to arrest certain native leaders for carrying on agitation against forced labour. The Government ordered the arrest of three men, who were to be flogged as a sort of warning to the others. The workers immediately protested, and declared a general strike. On this occasion the soldiers, most of whom were West African tribesmen, refused to obey their white officers, with the result that the agitators were freed and the Government ordered the director of the railroad to investigate the grievances of the workers in order to prevent the disruption of the railroad service which disorganised French trade for several weeks.

3. *Ruanda-Urandi*

In this territory, formerly a part of German East Africa but which was given to Belgium as a mandate of the League of Nations after the war, was the scene of a widespread revolt in 1929.

Negroes starved by the thousands after being plundered of their lands, other thousands dying in droves in the Central African swamps in their desperate trek for food, hundreds of others kidnapped and forced into slavery in the Katonga copper mines, and then a revolt of the Equatorial tribes sweeping through the jungle, until drowned in blood by British and Belgian imperialists—this is the story of a people fighting for freedom against great odds.

The British and Belgian censors at first successfully silenced the story of one of the largest Negro rebellions which the white imperialists in Africa have yet had to face.

The only news permitted to reach Europe were missionary reports that thousands of Negro men, women and children were fleeing famine conditions throughout the Eastern Belgian Congo, and that the still living bodies of hundreds had been devoured by hyenas as they fell. It is now known that these thousands of black toilers were fleeing the guns of the Belgian and British troops as well as the ravages of famine.

Immediately after Belgium acquired this mandated territory, following the lines of her traditional colonial policy, she carried out a wholesale confiscation of native lands. These lands were parcelled out among Belgian companies. Many Social-Democratic concessionaries also received their full share of the loot.

As a result of this plundering and kidnapping of the natives, the fields were not tilled and a famine broke out in the district of Ruanda. Although thousands of natives were affected, the Belgian colonial administrators had no assistance to offer. At the same time the British " Labour " Government, through its representative of Uganda, ordered all exports of food to the stricken area cut off. The situation of the natives quickly became more and more terrible. As the pangs of hunger began to mount, the spirit of rebellion swept from the Belgian Ruanda to British Uganda, where the neighbouring tribes on the frontier also rose up in arms.

Under the leadership of the " King " of Ruanda's daughter and a leader of the Wa-Tusi tribe, the starving and desperate natives everywhere carried on their revolt throughout the British and Belgian districts.

The first serious clash occurred at *Gatsolon,* where the native chiefs known to be friendly with the imperialist officials were killed outright, together with a number of Belgian soldiers and officials. Armed with all the appliances of modern warfare, the Belgian troops were rushed to suppress the rebellion, and against them the natives, armed only with spears and knives, were nevertheless able to hold out for several weeks.

Finally, the leaders of the revolt had to give in. They fled
through the swamps followed by the Belgian soldiers until they
reached the Uganda frontier.   There the British authorities arrested
them and handed them over to the Belgian pursuers.   The " King "
of Ruanda's brother was one of the prisoners taken and, together
with over a thousand tribesmen, shot.   After the insurrection the
British King's African Rifles and a Belgian regiment were stationed
in *Kiforte*, the centre of the revolt.

For the moment the uprising has been suppressed, but the movement for liberation of the native peoples of the Congo has received
a tremendous impetus from the rebellion.

4. *Lower Belgian Congo*

One of the most formidable anti-imperialist movements in Central
Africa broke out in the Belgian Congo.   This movement, not
unlike similar ones in other parts of the continent, is described
as of a semi-religous political character.   It was started by a man
named *Simon Kibangi*, a carpenter by trade, who rallied thousands
of natives in the Lower Congo by promising to deliver them from the
oppression of the Belgian imperialists.   Kibangi was converted
to the Baptist form of Christianity by missionaries who, as he
afterwards discovered, were merely the tools of the imperialists.
The first stage of agitation was conducted largely among the natives
who had become Christian converts, Kibangi appealing to them
to desert the religion of the whites and to organise their own church.
This immediately brought the workers into conflict with the
Government, because they refused to work on certain days in
order to devote their time to the new religious movement.   This
began to have a tremendous effect upon the industrial life of the
Congo, which is absolutely dependent on native labour.   Later
on the movement assumed more and more of a political character,
thanks to the influence of native students from the British and
French West African colonies, who had migrated to the Congo
in order to get clerical employment.   Many of these students were
arrested by the Belgian Government and deported from the country
on the grounds of spreading sedition among the Congo natives.
They also attempted to arrest Kibangi, who took refuge in a native
hut which was gallantly defended by his followers.   They drove the
soldiers away after a pitched battle, in the course of which several
workers and soldiers were killed.   This created a general panic
throughout the native settlement of *Kin-Shasha*, where machine
guns and military forces were stationed.   Moreover, Kibangi
was finally arrested and charged before a military court-martial
with attempting to organise the natives for the purpose of over-
throwing the Congo State.   Kibangi was condemned to death.
Nine others were given life imprisonment, two 20 years, one 5 years,
while a girl by the name of *Mandambi*, whom the Government
prosecutor characterised as the most revolutionary woman in

the Congo, was sentenced to 2 years' imprisonment. The sentences passed by the court merely inflamed the revolutionary spirit of the masses. Strikes broke out in all parts of the Congo. Business at Thiseville was so badly affected that the European merchants petitioned the home Government with the request that Kibangi should be publicly hanged. The natives threatened to massacre every white man if their leader was put to death. The situation between the natives and the European population reached a stage of open conflict, which was only appeased by commuting the sentence on Kibangi to life imprisonment and the quashing of the sentences upon several of the other leaders on the condition that they would leave the territory.

Despite all attempts to crush the revolutionary movement it continues to have great influence in the Congo, especially among the youth who are breaking away from tribal influence, thanks to their proletarisation and increasing class-consciousness.

According to the Paper News Agency " *Fides,*" *of November 1st*, 1930, a renewed wave of Kibangi propaganda broke out in *Mitadi*, in the Lower Congo, aiming at the natives' independence and hostility to the Christian missionaries and white capitalists. As a result of the natives' hostility even the medical service in this territory has had to be abandoned. The Brussels correspondent of the " African World " states that the present agitation is probably the result of propaganda carried out by Moscow agents and that the Government should immediately proclaim martial law and shoot on the spot the ring-leaders irrespective of race and nationality.

5. *Madagascar*

In this island there is also a well-developed anti-imperialist movement. In May, 1929, mass demonstrations were held under the leadership of Communists. Many of the demonstrators were arrested. In January, 1930, they were tried, and two of the Communist leaders were sentenced. On of them—*Plaoue*—was sentenced to 5½ years' and the other—*Vittori*—3½ years' imprisonment.

V.—HAITI

The underlying factors of the 1929 Haitian revolt against American imperialism, like the uprising in Nigeria, were : (1) the worsening of the conditions of the peasantry, due to the world crisis which has caused a falling of the prices of agricultural products, especially coffee ; (2) the expropriation of lands for the development of industrialised agriculture by American capitalists, and (3) the attempts on the part of the imperialists to force the natives to contribute labour for road building without pay.

As soon as the uprising occurred, martial law was proclaimed by Colonel Richards Coots, the American officer commanding marines in Port-au-Prince. The troops were immediately got in readiness, and bloody attacks were made against all those who participated in the uprising.

The first stage was a strike among the students of the National University. They held parades through the principal streets of Port-au-Prince, protesting against the educational bureaucracy saddled upon them by President Borneo and his American educational advisors. In order to cut down national expenses, the Government recently made a sweeping reduction in the education budget. So incensed are all sections of the population against the present fascist dictatorship that no sooner had the students walked out of their classes than the native staff in the Customs Department joined in the strike. The clerks attacked the American officials with ink bottles, parts of typewriters and other office accessories, chasing them out of the building. The dock workers also declared a general strike, and within a few hours the entire business life of the city of Port-au-Prince was at a standstill.

Thousands of Haitian workers gathered before the Government administration building and the President's palace, shouting *" DOWN WITH BORNEO !" " DOWN WITH AMERICAN IMPERIALISM !"*

The most serious manifestations, however, took place in the country districts. Because of their impoverished condition the peasants showed the most militancy. Immediately after learning what had taken place in the city they organised their forces and began a march on the capital.

Thousands of them gathered at a place called *Aux Cayes*, an important agricultural settlement. An advance guard of about 150 men and women armed with machetes (long knives used for cutting sugar canes) and sticks, marched ahead of the demonstrators. They were bent upon driving the American officials and their puppet, Borneo, out of Port-au-Prince.

As the column advanced on the capital, shouting *" DOWN WITH BORNEO !" " DOWN WITH FREEMAN !"* (who is the most vicious agent of American imperialism on the island, enjoying a salary of $10,000), they were met by a regiment of marines armed with every device of modern warfare.

The soldiers demanded that the peasants halt and return to their villages, which they refused to do. The marines then opened fire, killing five and wounding twenty. Despite the overwhelming superiority in numbers and equipment of the American forces, the natives fought heroically, making successful counter-attacks upon the military outposts at *Chatel* and *Torbecks*. By bringing up their reinforcements the peasants were able to break into the national guard-house at *St. Michael*, where they inflicted a severe assault on Lieutenant George Bertein, a Haitian petty-bourgeois renegade in the service of the American imperialists.

As the struggle increased more marines as well as American business men, who volunteered their services as a special fascist corps, were hurried off in armoured cars to various sections of the island to suppress the insurrection which was spreading from village to village.

While all this was taking place in the outskirts of the city, General Russell, the then High Commissioner, telegraphed to President Hoover informing him of the uprising. The American " dictator," who is fast adopting to himself the mantle of Mussolini, ordered the cruiser *Galveston*, then at its naval base in Cuba, to proceed to Haiti. The bombing plane, *Wright*, with 500 more marines, was also dispatched on its mission of " peace and goodwill."

With this formidable array the revolt was crushed with the same ruthlessness which characterised the marine campaigns in Nicaragua.

The reaction that has followed has created an atmosphere of widespread terrorism. Workers are afraid to express opposition sentiments for fear of being thrown into jail or murdered by the soldiers.

These outrages have aroused such world-wide protests among the working class and toiling masses of the colonies, especially in Latin-America, where Yankee imperialism rules supreme, that the Wall Street controlled Government in Washington was forced to dispatch a commission to "investigate" conditions. The Commissioners will merely carry out in the commission the instructions of their masters and whitewash the marine murderers of their bloody crimes, as has been done in the past.

The Haitian toilers know this only too well, and on the occasion of the arrival of the Commission at Port-au-Prince organised boycott demonstrations, demanding the immediate withdrawal of the marines and the abolition of the present dictatorship. The masses are still in a fighting mood. This was demonstrated when 5,000 workers and peasants shouting " LONG LIVE LIBERTY ! " held a protest meeting before the Government buildings.

Since this incident a number of minor skirmishes have occurred between the toilers and the police in different parts of the island. The Haitian toiling masses will carry on the struggle until their country is freed from marine rule and foreign domination.

VI.—WEST INDIES

There are also signs of unrest among the natives in the British West Indian colonies of Trinidad, Jamaica, Barbados, Grenada and British Guiana, the United States' Virgin Islands, and the French colonies of Martinique and Guadeloupe. In the British group of islands, a nationalist movement has already crystallised itself around the Labour Party of Trinidad and the left-wing intellectuals in the other islands. Monster mass meetings are being held throughout the islands, rallying together the workers and poor farmers under the slogan of " THE WEST INDIES FOR THE WEST INDIANS ! "

1. *Trinidad*

This unrest shows itself in a number of spontaneous strikes which have occurred in the various islands during recent years. The longshoremen's strike which took place in Trinidad some time ago marked the beginning of the rapid development of the trade union movement in that colony. Despite the weak leadership, reflected in the reformist programme and tactics of the labour leaders in Trinidad, the wide masses which strikes embrace show the potential forces of the Negro workers. For example, the longshoremen's strike occurred during one of the busy shipping seasons in the harbour of Port of Spain. The strike was called when the shipping companies (Royal Mail Steam Packet Co., Harrison Line, Lamport and Holt, Royal Netherlands, etc., etc.) threatened to cut down the wages of the men. The workers not only refused to handle freight but organised themselves into committees of action and marched through the city, where they closed down all the shipping firms until a settlement was arrived at. The military commander of troops, Colonel May, not confident as to the reaction of his garrison, refrained from provoking an armed uprising, despite the pressure brought to bear on the Government by the Chamber of Commerce to drive the workers from the streets, so as to enable the companies to conduct their shipping business.

These were memorable days in this slave outpost of the British slave Empire, for it was the first time that the young working class had entered into open struggle not only against the employers but against the State. However, after the strike was suppressed by naval marines landed from a British cruiser, most of the leaders were arrested. Some were imprisoned and others deported. The Government was able to carry out these reprisals simply because the petty-bourgeois reformist leaders who were at the head of the movement, when confronted with the necessity of leading the mass uprising, became timid and deserted the struggle. The workers, on the other hand, were unable to produce the necessary leadership to take charge of the situation and conduct a counter-offensive, for they had permitted the entire apparatus of the unions to be dominated by the reformists.

Since 1929, thanks to the severe agrarian crisis, expressed in the tremendous fall in the price of sugar, which has ruined the West Indian sugar planters, wide unrest is developing among the agricultural labourers. The first open outburst occurred in July, 1930.

According to a report which appeared in the Trinidad Press :
" Over 800 East Indians and Negroes, composed mainly of sugar field labourers from *Felicity State*, Chaguanas, and their sympathisers, assembled in Woodford Square, Port of Spain. Their object, it was stated, was to show the Government their dissatisfaction with the labour conditions on that estate.

" Six of the number formed a deputation which demanded action from the Government.

" The trouble began a week ago, when a large body of the labourers on Felicity estate struck. They complained that the task work allotted them had been increased, and asked either for a return to the old task measurements or increased wages.

" There was reported to be considerable unrest, but the prompt though pacific action of the police prevented an armed demonstration from assuming ugly proportions.

" It is understood that a compromise was effected on the basis that the old tasks would be adopted. But this decision was not endorsed by the estate authorities, and the trouble started afresh.

" The Government Commission of Labour together with the employers assured the workers that their demands would be granted. However, when they returned to the plantation all the promises made to them were broken ; they were disarmed and their leaders arrested and charged with rioting. Shortly after this incident another strike occurred on one of the the big sugar plantations in the Caroni District in Trinidad. The workers destroyed much property and drove all of the native overseers and European superintendents away from the plantation. The situation was only brought under control after large squads of armed police were despatched to the scene of the trouble."

The general conditions of the toiling masses are becoming worse and worse daily. With the closing down of the big sugar factories as well as the curtailment in oil production—one of the basic industries in Trinidad—thousands of workers are being thrown out of employment.

2. Barbados

On the occasion of the visit of Lord Olivier, one of the leaders of the British " Labour " Party, who acted as the chairman of the Committee to inquire into the sugar industry in the British West Indies in 1930, the Negro workers in Barbados organised protest demonstrations demanding the abolition of their present semi-serf conditions, their right to the franchise and their right to free lands which are at present monopolised by small groups of white colonial autocrats and absentee English landlords. Among these is the Earl of Harewood, the son-in-law of King George the Fifth. This shows how the remnants of the English feudal nobility have entrenched themselves on the colonial toilers. Lord Olivier,with all the hypocrisy characteristic of a social-fascist, frowned upon the demands of the black workers, and only interested himself in putting forward the demands of the sugar planters for imperial subsidy in order to enable them to continue their exploitation of the Negro and East Indian workers. The natives, however, are becoming more and more class-conscious, and have already created their own trade union and political organisation, in order to carry on the struggle against their imperialist oppressors.

3. Jamaica

In Jamaica, a colony where the natives have tremendous re-volutionary traditions (the Maroon rebellions of the eighteenth century and of 1865), the workers are beginning to form trade union and political organisations. The recent strikes (1929 and 1930) have created such alarm that the Government has ordered the native regiment to be disbanded, replacing it by British soldiers, because they fear that in the event of a national uprising native soldiers would fraternise with the toiling masses.

American imperialism, through the United Fruit Company, one of the biggest corporations operating in Latin America and the West Indies, is dealing a death blow to the British interests in the banana industry in Jamaica. This rivalry has had a tremendous effect in worsening the conditions of the Jamaican blacks, who, however, are using the strike weapon with much success. A number of political strikes took place among the dock and transport workers in 1930, resulting in armed clashes between the workers and the police, who are natives under the command of European officers.

One of the clashes with the police took place at Rio Cabre, near *Spanish Town*. The Government is constructing a bridge there and employing labour at 3/– per day. A few weeks after work began, the men, realising how badly they were being exploited, formed a strike committee and downed tools. They demanded eight hours labour at 3/6 per day instead of 3/–. The employers (Government contractors) refused and the men began to picket the bridge. The Government ordered armed police to the scene, and attempted to break the strike through intimidation. The labourers refused to return to work under the old conditions. Strike-breakers were brought in, and the strikers took active measures to see that the blacklegs did not work. Then the police sided with the strike-breakers, and a general pitched battle took place. The police used their rifles and bayonets, while the strikers kept up the offensive with bottles and stones. Only after reinforcement was rushed to the scene were the strikers outnumbered and dispersed by the superior arms of the police.

The Jamaica Trades and Labour Union, which was organised in 1929 through the activities of the revolutionary Trade Union Unity League and the Negro Labour Congress in America, is taking the leadership in the class struggles of the toiling masses. Branches have been established in the most important industrial areas of the island. Special attention is being paid to the organisation of the agricultural workers, especially those employed in the banana industry.

4. French Colonies

In the French island of Guadeloupe the labour situation is also becoming very tense. In February, 1930, the workers in one of the largest sugar factories declared a strike demanding shorter hours and an increase in wages.   Several clashes took place between the strikers and the gendarmerie (police) which resulted in the death of three strikers and two policemen.   Four other workers were also badly wounded by police gun-fire.

The strike lasted for several days.   Auxiliary divisions of gendarmerie from the neighbouring islands of *Martinique* were brought in to help suppress the strike.   There is much agitation among the agricultural labourers, who are being more and more victimised because of the crisis which exists in the sugar industry.   The sugar manufacturers and plantation owners are attempting to throw the burden on the backs of the workers by cutting down wages and increasing hours.

VII.—THE UNITED STATES

The revolutionary spirit among the Negro toilers is not only confined to the black colonial masses, but is also manifesting itself among the Negro proletariat in the United States.

Thanks to the economic crisis, which has worsened the standard of living of these workers to a very marked degree, the Negro masses are becoming more and more radicalized.   This leftward swing of the Negro masses is bringing them into closer and closer alliance with the class-conscious white workers under the leadership of the *Communist Party and Trade Union Unity League,* the revolutionary trade union centre in the U.S.A.   In order to break up this alliance between the whites and blacks, and thereby weaken the counter-offensive of the workers against the capitalists, the bourgeoisie, with the aid of their social-fascist lackeys of the Socialist Party and the American Federation of Labour, as well as the open fascist organisations like the *Ku Klux Klan,* the *Black Shirts,* the *American Legion,* etc., have launched a new wave of white terror (lynching) against the Negro masses.   The bourgeoisie hope that, by playing up social prejudice and inciting lynchings and race riots, they will be able to distract the attention of the workers from their common class interests in fighting against the widespread misery and starvation.   The Negro workers are showing their determination not to permit themselves to be led astray and thereby breaking up the united front between themselves and the white workers against their oppressors.

The most striking expressions of solidarity between the toilers of both races are to be seen in the united struggles of the Unemployed.

For example, on the 6th of March, 1930, the first *International Day of Struggle against Unemployment,* organised and led by the Communist Party and the T.U.U.L., thousands of Negro workers not only participated in the monster demonstrations which took place in all the big industrial centres of the country, but played a leading rôle.

Since then the Negro workers, together with their class-conscious white allies, have carried on repeated struggles in various parts of the United States. A demonstration of over three thousand workers, about two-thirds Negroes, took place in Birmingham, Alabama, on December 21st, 1930, under militant slogans demanding work or relief.

The same applied to the Hunger March which took place in Toledo, Ohio, on December 22nd, 1930—while in Charlotte, North Carolina, and Denver, Colorado, thousands of Negro and white workers carried on militant struggles against the police who attempted to break up their demonstration. In the course of all these demonstrations the police and other capitalist agents have directed most vicious attacks upon the blacks, in order to break up the inter-racial solidarity and to intimidate the Negroes from taking an active part in the struggles of their class.

Apart from these joint struggles of the white and black unemployed, the Negroes themselves have organised many spontaneous strikes and demonstrations. In Chicago, Negro women, by means of a successful campaign of picketing white capitalist enterprises (Woolworth Stores) won the right to be employed in places that attempted to discriminate against them. Spontaneous manifestations of struggle are becoming widespread in the South. In Georgia, Tennessee, Alabama, etc., Negro tenants and farm labourers are breaking into the warehouses of the white farmers and landlords and helping themselves to food. Agricultural workers in Tennessee called a number of strikes in 1930. The same applies to New Orleans, where Negro dockers went on a spontaneous strike. Besides these cases of spontaneous demonstrations, there has been a wave of resistance by the Negro workers in the South in the form of armed defence. Landlords attempting to terrorise Negroes and attack them and their families have been shot. In December, 1930, an unemployed demonstration of 300 Negroes with banners " *We want work or food* " was organised in Shreveport, Louisiana, which developed into a clash between the workers and the police. Wherever we turn in America to-day we find an increasing spirit of revolutionary consciousness among the Negro masses.

PART III

CHAPTER V

BLACK SOLDIERS OF IMPERIALISM

I.—THE WAR DANGER

THERE is imminent danger of another imperialist war and an armed attack of the capitalist states upon the Soviet Union. Plans for these were glaringly revealed during the trial of the counter-revolutionists in Moscow in December,1930, and March,1931. The anti-Soviet plotters confessed that they were the agents of the French imperialists in preparing for the intervention and destruction of the first workers' State. It is necessary to point out the economic and political reasons why war is being prepared, and the extent to which the imperialists are militarising their black colonial slaves for use when war begins.

In the first place, the present deep crisis of the world capitalist system signalises a renewed attack against the already miserable existence of the Negro masses.

The crisis finds its reflection in the acute rivalry among the imperialist nations in their struggle for the re-division of the world, which must inevitably culminate in an imperialist war.

While the capitalist world is on the decline, the Soviet Union is developing and successfully building a Socialist Society. The workers, and peasants of the Soviet Union, after the victorious overthrow of the capitalist system in their country in 1917, have since become the fortress of the revolutionary workers throughout the world. The Soviet Union is the only country that knows no oppression, knows no exploitation, has no imperialists aims and supports the revolutionary liberation movements of the workers and toiling peasants of all countries as well as the emancipatory struggles of the Negro toiling masses for self-determination.

To the capitalist world engulfed in crisis the Soviet Union, which is successfully constructing its socialist industry on the basis of the great Five Year Plan and raising the cultural level and the economic conditions of the more backward nationalities within its territory to higher level, has become the primary object of attack. Hence the bitter hatred of the imperialists to the Soviet Union which reveals itself in their campaigns of lies and slander about "religious persecution," "Soviet dumping," and "forced labour," all of which is being done for the purpose of creating animosity among the more backward sections of the workers in the capitalist countries, so that they could be mobilized as cannon fodder against the Soviet Union.

It is also important for every Negro toiler to note the increasing armament race going on now between the imperialist nations, while at the same time the imperialists are organising " disarmament conferences " in order to give the workers the belief that they are striving for peace. It must be distinctly understood that the result of each such conference was the further increase in the war budgets of the imperialist nations. (London Disarmament Conference.)

In connection with the war preparations, the practice of dividing the black and white workers, of pitting one against the other on grounds of race—a policy which is the mainstay of imperialist oppression—is now being intensified. The Hertzog Native Bills in South Africa, the new wave of lynching and mob violence now taking place in the United States against the Negroes, and organised by the imperialists, is aimed towards widening the artificial barrier between the black and the white workers, as well as the international working class as a whole.

In order to carry out their war plans, the capitalists are also preparing reserve *black armies*. The reason for this is obvious. The imperialists, especially the French, the leaders of the anti-Soviet military campaign, are afraid that their European armies, which are made up of workers, peasants and toiling youth, will refuse to execute the orders of the bourgeoisie to attack the Soviet Union, the fatherland of the working class. So, in order to guarantee the carrying out of their plans, the French imperialists are mobilising one of the largest black armies in Africa which could be brought to Europe and used as shock troops when the war begins. At the present moment these African troops are being freely used in suppressing colonial revolts both in Africa and in Asia, as well as strikes in France. Furthermore, in the event of a proletarian uprising in France or other European countries, black colonial troops will be utilised to crush the revolution instead of white soldiers.

During the period of the World War, over 200,000 African natives served in the French Army. The majority of these men were recruited under the direction of *Blaise Diagne*, a Senegalese Negro politician who was commissioned by Poincaré as the special representative of French imperialism in Africa during the war. Since then Diagne has been closely identified with the war plans of his imperialist masters, who in order to draw him still closer to them recently made him Assistant Minister for the Colonies in the Laval Government. This has been done to create the impression among the Negro petty-bourgeoisie and intellectuals that the French imperialists are liberal, while their true aim is to use Diagne's prestige to carry on war preparations in the African colonies.

Despite the fact that the policy of militarising Negroes is most developed in the French colonies, it must be stated that all imperialist powers are also training black soldiers for future wars. This applies especially to the United States, Great Britain and Belgium.

Although there is no compulsory military service in the United States, the Negro workers are nevertheless coerced by their employers to take up military training during the summer months in the Citizens' Military Training Camps. Those who fail to attend these military courses are dismissed from their jobs. Through this method of industrial terrorism, thousands of Negro youths are being trained to take their place in the trenches to fight for their capitalist exploiters. The capitalists are now appealing to the unemployed to join the army as a solution for the unemployed problem. This applies especially to the young workers.

Furthermore, the United States Government also provides for the training of reserve officers among the sons of the Negro bourgeoisie and petty-bourgeoisie who attend certain colleges and universities. For example, *Howard University* in Washington, D.C., as well as *Hampton College*, in Virginia, receive money grants from the Federal Government and instructors from the War Department for preparing the Negro youth to lead the workers and peasants of their race to slaughter. All students are compelled to study military science for two years. Those who refuse are either expelled or denied the right of receiving their diplomas.

The following facts briefly indicate the extent to which the Negro toilers have been mobilised and used by various imperialist powers.

II.—Origin of French African Army

(*a*) In the early part of the 19th century France began the militarisation of her black colonial natives by the sending of certain tribes on punitive expeditions to subjugate other recalcitrant tribes. This process of militarisation has been developed to such a degree that France may be taken as a classical example of the present day military policy of the imperialist nations in Africa.

The following is a chronological table showing the military policy of France prior to the World War.

In 1828 two companies of *Ouolofs* were sent to Madagascar to subjugate the natives there.

In 1838 one company of *Senegalese* was sent to the Guinea Coast. Troops were further used in the Crimean War and in the war with Mexico.

In 1870 African troops fought in the Franco-Prussian War. Senegalese troops were used to subjugate West and Equatorial Africa.

In 1912 Senegalese troops were utilised in the Moroccan War. They were also used in the Madagascar campaigns.

(b) *War Decrees and Commissions Prior to the World War.*—In 1904 a decree issued provided for the recruitment of native soldiers in West Africa, and in case sufficient soldiers could not be raised, conscription be resorted to.

In 1907, as a result of a Government commission appointed to study the recruitment of natives in West Africa, conscription was introduced. Senegal troops were later sent to North Africa as a garrison.

In 1910 another commission was appointed to investigate the question of conscription in West Africa. The commission concluded that it was possible to secure 40,000 men annually for a period of 5 years in West Africa, but that only a fifth of this number would be needed.

In 1912 a decree was enacted making possible the creation of a large black army. Under this decree, natives between the ages of 20 and 28 could be conscripted for a term of 4 years. Before the war the Government annually recruited between 8,000 and 10,000 men.

(c) *During the World War and After.*—*October*, 1915—30,000 men (volunteers and conscripts) were recruited to be sent to Europe.

On October 9th, 1915, a decree was enacted which made provision for the enlistment of natives over 18 years old in the Senegalese Corps, to serve outside French West Africa for the period during the war. The time thus served was deducted from the compulsory service which these natives might later be called upon to perform in the colonies. Each native upon enlisting would receive 200 francs.

The Government recruited 51,000 more men in 1916, nearly one-half of whom came from Senegal and the Sudan.

In 1917 there were 31 Senegalese battalions on the Somme.

January, 1918.—A decree was issued which extended the age of recruits from 18 to 35 years, and the system which heretofore had been applied only to West Africa was extended to Equatorial Africa. This decree further authorised universal conscription.

Six additional decrees issued in 1918 gave native soldiers a number of privileges, such as exemption from certain forms of taxation, and granting them under certain circumstances citizenship. Provision was made for the payment of allowances to the families of soldiers. Agricultural and medical schools, and a sanatorium for invalid soldiers were authorised, to be established in each colony. Certain employments in the Government service were likewise reserved for ex-soldiers. All these gestures were made in order to facilitate recruitment and pacify the unrest which was taking place among the natives in the French colonies who were revolting against forced military service.

By granting the franchise and citizenship to the soldiers, thus raising their status above the other toiling masses, France created a buffer group which could be used as the direct tools of the im-

perialists to foster their sinister aims.   These concessions tended
to create artificial differentiations among the masses during the
World War, and since then have accelerated the development of
class lines.

A special decree enacted in 1919 fixed the term of military
service for native "subjects" in French West Africa and Equatorial
Africa for three years.

In 1923 the term of military service for " citizens " in France
was reduced to 18 months, but the term for " subjects " remained
the same.   The black " citizens " spend their 18 months in Senegal,
but the " subjects " are sent to France, where the likelihood of
death is much greater, due to climatic conditions.   Natives
physically unfit for regular military service are obliged to serve
in labour battalions.

(d) *Policy in the Mandated Territories.*—In the *Cameroons* and
Togoland there are no organised military forces except for local
police purposes and for defence.   But in case of war the troops
raised for defence may be used outside of the local territory.

France may conscript the natives of those two mandated territories,
notwithstanding the terms of the League of Nations mandate,
for already as early as 1920 the natives of the Cameroons were
subjected to the conscription laws of Equatorial Africa. Natives
are still being enlisted in the battalions in the mandated territories.
These troops are under the control of the commandants of the
West and Equatorial African military forces.

A decree enacted on June 25th, 1925, gave Togo and the Cameroons
complete autonomy from the military point of view.   It provides
that the military organisation of these two territories shall consist
of units of native militia, who together with the native guard and
the interior police are responsible for the security of these territories.
This decree specifically abrogates the decree of 1920 which attached
the military forces of the Cameroons to West and Equatorial
Africa.

Since January, 1925, the military organisation of the Cameroons
has consisted of native militia (4 companies, 2 stationed in the North
and 2 in the South, composed of 15 French officers, 36 non-commissioned officers, and 656 native soldiers).

The Native Guard consists of 894 native police.

In Togo there is no native militia, but a native guard of 400
members.

(e) *Present System of Conscription.*—In 1919 the West African
quota of soldiers was fixed at 23,000 annually.   In West Africa
125,000 to 130,000 men annually come of recruiting age, but
because of physical unfitness only 10,000 men are conscripted
annually.

In 1926, 10,000 natives were furnished for foreign military
service.

(f) Contingents from the various French African Colonies :

Upper Volta ...	2,500	Ivory Coast	...	1,500
Sudan	2,000	Dahomey	...	800
Senegal ...	1,700	Niger		700
Guinea ...	1,850	Mauretania	...	100

The native soldiers receive about one dollar a month and serve a period of three years. They receive three months' instruction, after which they are sent in detachments of 600 to France, accompanied by one doctor. After three months' instruction in France they are then assigned to companies and sent to *Morocco, Algeria, Syria* or *Indo-China.*

At present there are 40,000 native soldiers. Of this number, 20,000 are stationed in West Africa, the remainder in France and various colonies. In addition, France maintains a local police force of about 15,000 men in her West African colonies. The West African troops are divided into 20 regiments of 2,000 men each.

In 1926, 14,000 men were sent to fight in Morocco against Abdul-Krim. Permanent black troops are stationed in the following French colonies :

Algeria	...	...	4,000
Morocco	...	...	4,000
Tunis	...	...	4,000
Syria	...	...	2,000

besides an additional 2,000 in each colony in the Federation. In the Sudan and Senegal several regiments are garrisoned. The West African Government contributes about 7,500,000 francs annually to the military budget.

(g) Mortality.—The mortality rate is very high among black troops, due to pulmonary affections, syphilis, malaria and other maladies. Nearly 82.32 per cent. of Senegalese stationed in Europe contracted tuberculosis. Thanks to the persistent opposition of the natives to conscription and the bad conditions under which the Negroes are forced to live, conscription is being applied only in Niger and Mauretania for the present. Furthermore, conscription in French West Africa has given rise to mass revolts and migrations of the natives to the surrounding territories, such as the Gold Coast, Nigeria, Gambia, Sierra Leone and Liberia.

In 1924, 17,000 out of 126,000 eligibles were " bons absents."

In 1924, one-third of the natives in Upper Volta were " bons absents."

In 1925, 4,668 Senegalese were " bons absents."

In several instances martial law has been declared in order to conduct the recruitment, so widespread has been the opposition to militarisation.

Since the war, growing resistance of the Negroes to conscription and the whole militarist policy of the imperialists in the colonies in general, together with the inhuman French economic methods of exploitation, found its sharpest expression in the uprising of the natives in French Equatorial Africa in November, 1928, which lasted for several months.

III.—British Colonial Troops

1. *Anglo-Belgian Native Troops*

These troops were used in joint action by the British and Belgian imperialists during the East African campaigns in 1914-1917.

The Uganda Transport Corps (Carrier Section):

Carriers and Stretcher Bearers	38,310
Medical Detachment	844
Headmen, etc.	149
Ox Transport (Belgian)	161
,, ,, (U.T.C.)	152
Maxim Gun-Porters	149
Sycos	114
Veterinary details	49
Telegraphs	38
Supply	38
Pioneers	25
The E.A. Carrier Corps—Porters	3,576
,, Congo ,, ,, ,, ...	8,429
Belgian Military Telegraph Construction ...	500
Uganda Pioneers	500

Carriers supplied for operations in German East Africa were 5,763.

South Africa maintains a police force with a few natives on the staff. In 1923 the total number of native, coloured and Indian police were 3,845.

In all four provinces of South Africa natives are excluded from military training. Because of the developing revolutionary movement in South Africa, led by the Communist Party, the bourgeoisie are afraid to teach the natives to use arms. The only way in which the capitalists have been able to maintain domination over the blacks is by disarming them, and arming the entire white bourgeois and petty-bourgeois sections of the population.

In January, 1927, a Bill was passed providing for the compulsory enrolment of all white residents between the ages of 18 and 50 both of whose parents must be European. This Bill excludes the Natives, who are thereby unable to defend themselves against fascist mobs which periodically attack their residential quarters in Durban and other towns.

2. *East and West Africa*

The *King's African Rifles* is the military organisation of British East Africa. A similar army known as the West African Frontier Force exists in British West Africa. The King's African Rifles now consists of four battalions of 4,000 men. One battalion is stationed in Uganda, one in Nyassaland, and two in Tanganyika. According to the terms of the League of Nations mandate, the Tanganyika Government may not "organise any native military forces in the territory except for local police purposes and for the defence of the territory." Nevertheless, black troops are being maintained on regular army basis. A special battalion composed of natives is supported by the Tanganyika Government.

The West African Frontier Force was organised as early as 1900. They are stationed through the colonies of Gambia, Sierra Leone, Gold Coast and Nigeria. All of the officers in East and West Africa are British army men.

3. *The West Indies and South America*

(a) The *Bahamas* have no military force. There is a local force consisting of police whose duties are of a semi-military nature. It consists of two officers, 112 ranks, armed with S.M.L.E. rifles. The headquarters are at Nassau. The officers are Europeans, but the rank and file Negroes, 60 per cent. of whom are recruited from Barbados. Enlistment is for six years.

(b) *Barbados.*—The local force consists of the following units :

> Barbados Volunteer Force.
> Volunteer Reserves.
> Cadet Corps and Brigade.
> Barbados Rifle Association.
> Barbados police force liable to military service.

The Cadet Corps and Brigade are composed of boys over 12.

(c) *Bermuda.*—The local force consists of :

Militia	Enlistment for six years.
Volunteer	Only whites admitted.
Cadets	Semi-military.

(d) *British Guiana.*—The local force consists of :

Military forces	Militia (Artillery, Infantry and Reserves).
Police	British Guiana Police.

The police are liable for military service.

Every male person who is a British subject between 18 and 45 years old is also liable for war service.

The artillery is composed exclusively of European colonists.

In the infantry one platoon is composed of Europeans and

Creoles (Mulattoes) and the other platoons, Creoles (Mulattoes) and Negroes. The men are enlisted for three years.

(e) *British Honduras.*—The local force consists of a military force and police. The police are also liable for military service. The men are principally natives of the colony and British West Indies. Enlistment is for three years. Men between 18 and 45 years are eligible for service. Police consist of natives of the colony who enlist for one year.

(f) *Jamaica.*—Local force consists of a military force and police. The officers are Europeans, the ranks consist of natives.

(g) *Leeward Island.*—Officers are Europeans. The ranks are composed of coloured and black West Indians.

(h) *Trinidad.*—Military force and police (constabulary), which is liable for military service.

(i) *Windward Islands.*—The military force consists of:
St. Lucia Volunteer Corps, liable for service within the colony only. Headquarters at Castries. Men who are natives of the West Indies (Negro or Mulatto) enlist for three years.

(j) *St. Vincent.*—Volunteer Corps for military service within the colony only. Men who enlist for three years are either white, black or coloured West Indians.

Police are liable for military service.

During the last war a special West Indian Regiment was recruited for service in France, Palestine and the East African campaigns.

IV.—NEGRO TROOPS OF THE UNITED STATES OF AMERICA

The following table shows the number of Negro troops used during past wars.

(a) Spanish-American War ...   ...   Over 10,000.
(b) War with Philippines   ...   ...   About 4,000.
(c) In 1910—War with Mexico   ...   Two Negro Regiments.

World War—From June 5th, 1917 to Sept. 12th, 1918, about 2,290,527 Negroes were registered for military service in Europe. Of this number 72.60 per cent. were accepted.

The number inducted into service was 367,710. The number accepted for full military service was 342,277, including those in the regular army and national guard, which amounted to about 380,000. Approximately 200,000 were sent to France.

V.—THE CONGO ARMY

The first native army in the Congo Free State was recruited as early as 1885. By means of this force, Leopold was able to compel the natives to collect rubber and to impose his rule on the blacks. Before 1900 the term of enlistment was five years, but in 1900 it was extended to seven years. The soldiers received 21 centimes per day.

At present the force consists of 13,000 men. The soldiers are paid 30 centimes a day, and this sum is increased to 45 centimes upon re-enlistment.

In 1926 the annual quota was fixed at 5,040. When there are not sufficient volunteers the Government resorts to conscription.

In the Belgian Congo the police and military forces are combined, while in French and British territories these two forces are maintained separately. Furthermore, there are about 15 soldiers for every 10,000 inhabitants as compared with Tanganyika and Uganda, where the ratio is ten and twelve respectively.

PART IV

CHAPTER VI

REVOLUTIONARY PERSPECTIVES

I.—THE ROLE OF THE R.I.L.U. IN THE STRUGGLES OF
THE NEGRO WORKERS

THE Red International of Labour Unions (Profintern) celebrated its Tenth Anniversary in 1930. Having been organised in the very heat of the acute post-war economic and political crisis in the most important European countries, the Profintern came to be the militant revolutionary headquarters of the world trade union movement, rallying to its banner all the class-conscious proletarian elements of the whole world.

To-day the Profintern is in the thick of its struggle for winning over the working class. In spite of its fine successes in extending its influence the Profintern cannot yet say that it embraces the majority of the working class. The Profintern is still obliged to wage a relentless struggle for freeing the workers from the influence of the bourgeoisie, the reformists and anarcho-syndicalists. The greatest enemy of the Profintern in the struggle for influence over the working class is the International Trade Union Federation, the so-called Amsterdam International.

The Amsterdam International was organised one year prior to the Profintern. In spite of its high-sounding name of " International Federation," Amsterdam is, in the main, an association of European trade unions, owing to the fact that out of the 28 organisations affiliating with it 23 are in Europe and only 5 organisations are non-European. Besides, the Amsterdam International is a white chauvinist international. The Amsterdamites reflect the interests of the upper strata of the working class in the imperialist countries, and look down upon the trade union movement of the colonial and coloured peoples. Amsterdam's first and most important task is to preserve and reinforce capitalism and imperialism, and to strengthen the position of the bourgeoisie by suppressing the revolutionary movement in the imperialist countries and the national liberation movements in the colonies and semi-colonial countries.

The Profintern is the first real International of Trade Unions, because the workers of all nationalities and races, regardless of

colour or creed, have rallied to its banner. The Profintern has its
sections in practically all countries in the world, in the form of
independent trade unions and opposition groups and minorities
inside the reformist trade unions. Besides these trade unions,
which are organisationally connected with the Profintern, there are
a whole number of trade union federations which adhere to the
ideological leadership of the Profintern. Two very powerful
organisations are among these—the Pan-Pacific Trade Union Secretariat and the Latin-American Confederation of Labour.

The Red International of Labour Unions is the first Trade Union
International which furthered the development of the trade union
movement among the colonial peoples, and succeeded in rallying
a great part of them to its banner. It is the only international
which conducts a consistent and permanent struggle against white
chauvinism, for equal rights for the labour movement in the
colonial and semi-colonial countries, for the correct solution of the
national-race problem. This struggle has only just begun. The
problem of national equality has not been sufficiently appraised
even by many of the Profintern supporters, while in the ranks of
those sections of the working class which still follow the reformist
and the reactionary leadership the " race struggle " in most cases,
we regret to say, overshadows the class struggle. The Profintern
has, however, mapped out a correct line for solving the national-
race problem. It has indicated the path for waging the struggle
against race chauvinism, against all colour bars, for uniting the
workers of all races and nations.

A very vivid example of the national-race policy of the Profintern is its fight for strengthening and extending the trade union
movement among the Negro workers. The Negro workers are
the most exploited, the most oppressed in the world. It was the
fate of the Negro workers to pay the horrible tribute to slavery,
which served to destroy millions upon millions of black toilers.
The Negro workers even now are actually slave-bound to their
white conquerors. Different forms of forced labour, peonage,
expropriation of their lands, extraordinary laws and unbearably
heavy taxes, lynchings, segregation, etc., etc., are up till now the
fate of the Negro toiling masses languishing under the yoke of
imperialism. Tens of thousands of Negro workers are still groaning
under the lash of their enslavers.

The Negro workers, however, exploited and oppressed by the
imperialists, have not received the necessary support of the organised
labour movement. The white worker, in many cases even to-day,
still regards the Negro as a pariah, and scornfully refuses to stretch
out a helping hand to his black brother. Even in the ranks of the
revolutionary workers numerous examples of white chauvinism
can be recorded. A long and bitter struggle has been waged by
the Profintern against this psychology of " white superiority."
Day in and day out, year after year, the Profintern has raised the

Negro problem before its affiliated sections in the U.S.A., South Africa, England, France, Belgium, Portugal, etc., sharply condemning any and all manifestations of white chauvinism and underestimation of winning the black workers for the class struggle, pointing out the necessity of paying the most serious attention to the organisation of the Negro workers into revolutionary trade unions together with the white workers.

In order to strengthen and stimulate trade union activities among the Negro masses, the Profintern finally established a Negro Trade Union Committee composed of Negro workers from the United States, South, East, West and Equatorial Africa, the British and French West Indies and Latin America.

Since the establishment of the Committee, the Profintern has to some extent succeeded in overcoming white chauvinism in its ranks, and has corrected the mistakes of its American section, which formerly ignored work among the Negroes. The Profintern will continue its fight until it completely eradicates all traces of white chauvinism from its ranks and unites all workers—white black, yellow, brown—in one revolutionary trade union movement.

II.—What must be Done ?

In order to help the Profintern and its revolutionary trade union sections in the United States and South Africa to carry out the task of building up strong unions by strengthening the bonds of solidarity between the white and black workers, two things must be done.

(1) The class-conscious white workers must take the initiative of drawing the Negro workers into the revolutionary unions and the movement of the unemployed, guaranteeing to them every opportunity of actively participating in shaping the policies of the workers' organisations and leading the united front struggles of the working class against the offensive of the capitalists.

In this connection it is the special task of the revolutionary unions to bring the white workers into the struggle on behalf of the Negro demands. It must be borne in mind that the Negro masses will not be won for the revolutionary struggles until such time as the most conscious section of the white workers show, by action, that they are fighting with the Negroes against all racial discrimination and persecution. Every class-conscious worker must bear in mind that the age-long oppression of the colonial and weak nationalities by the imperialist powers has given rise to a feeling of bitterness among the masses of the enslaved countries, as well as a feeling of distrust toward the oppressing nation in general and toward the proletariat of those nations. This point was particularly emphasised in the resolution of the Communist International on the Negro Question in U.S.A.

It is absolutely necessary to pursue this policy. No retreat before white chauvinism must be tolerated, for only by *deeds and not words* will we be able to dispel the distrust which the more backward sections of the Negro toiling masses have towards the whites, a suspicion which has developed among them as a result of the traditional policy of the white reformist trade union leaders (Green, Mathew Woll, John L. Lewis, etc.). These A.F. of L. fakers not only refuse to organise the Negroes, but, when compelled to do so in order to safeguard the privileged position of the white labour aristocrats, invariably " Jim-Crow " the Negroes into separate unions and leave them at the mercy of the capitalists.

Furthermore, the white workers must realise that in the present condition of world capitalism one of the aims of the imperialists is to find a way out of their difficulties by using the Negro workers, especially in the colonies, to worsen the already low standard of the white workers. Because of this the struggles of the Negro workers against the capitalist offensive must be made part and parcel of the common struggle against imperialism.

The emancipation of the white workers from the yoke of capitalism can only be achieved by making a decisive break with all reformist tendencies, which are the ideologies of the bourgeoisie within the ranks of the working class. They must come forward boldly in support of the programme of the Communist International and the R.I.L.U., which alone struggle for the overthrow of capitalism and the liberation of the toiling masses of all races and colour.

The workers of the imperialist countries must not forget the memorable words of Marx that " labour in the white skin cannot free itself while labour in the black is enslaved."

(2) The Negro workers must also take a more active part in the revolutionary struggles of the working class as a whole. They must make a decisive break with all bourgeois and petty-bourgeois reformist movements. They must not permit themselves to be misled by the " left " phrases of the American Negro petty-bourgeois reformists, such as Du Bois, Moton, Depriest, etc., etc., who are merely office-seekers and demagogues paid by the ruling class to befuddle the Negro masses in order to direct their attention away from revolutionary struggle into reformist channels.

The Negro workers must also conduct a more relentless struggle against the Negro trade union lackeys of the reformists, whose chief task is to betray the struggles of the Negroes on the economic front. This has been glaringly revealed both in the U.S.A. and in South Africa. For example, A. Phillip Randolph and his hench-man, Frank Croswaith, " leaders " of the Pullman Porters' Union and members of the Socialist Party, are the most outstanding examples of Negro reformists. Some years ago the Pullman Porters' Union was the biggest mass organisation among Negro workers, but thanks to the opportunist policies pursued by Randolph and his supporters the organisation is almost bankrupt. To-day it is largely a dues-paying organisation and sick and death benefit society, completely under the domination of the bureaucrats of the A.F. of L., whose last act of betrayal of the Negro workers was openly to sabotage their struggles against the Pullman Company in 1928.

The same rôle of treachery has been played by the Negro reformists and other mis-leaders in the Union of South Africa. The natives must therefore conduct a sharper struggle against the tactics of Kadalie and Champion, as well as Ballinger, the British I.L.P. leader, who are the chief disrupters and splitters of the working-class movement among the blacks.

These agents of Amsterdam can boast of an unparalleled record of betrayals of the struggles of the natives of South Africa. The most recent example of Kadalie's hypocrisy was during the railroad strike in East London in 1930. After hundreds of native railroad workers downed tools and went out on strike Kadalie entered into a secret conference with the agents of the Government, who owned the railroads, and then appealed to the men to go back in order that they might get a few shillings to pay their dues from which Kadalie could secure his salary.

Again during the heroic struggles of the natives on Dingaan's Day (December 16th, 1930) Kadalie and Champion attempted to sabotage the demonstrations of the workers, who openly fought with the police for the right to protest against the vicious slave laws of the Hertzog's Government by burning their passes at monster mass meetings. Kadalie told the workers to be submissive and obey their oppressors. He promised to send a petition to Hertzog asking him to abolish the Pass laws, failing which he would call upon the workers to demonstrate in 1934. This shows the bankruptcy of Kadalie & Company.

The struggle against Garveyism represents one of the major tasks of the Negro toilers in America and the African and West Indian colonies.

Why must we struggle against Garveyism ? As the " Programme of the Communist International " correctly states : " Garveyism is a dangerous ideology which bears not a single democratic trait, and which toys with the aristocratic attributes of a non-existent ' Negro kingdom ' ! It must be strongly resisted, for it is not a help but a hindrance to the mass Negro struggle for liberation against American imperialism."

Garvey is more than a dishonest demagogue who, taking advantage of the revolutionary wave of protest of the Negro toilers against imperialist oppression and exploitation, was able to crystallise a mass movement in America in the years immediately after the war. His dishonesty and fraudulent business schemes, such as the *Black Star Line*, through which he extorted millions and millions of dollars out of the sweat of the Negro working class, soon led to his imprisonment. After his release Garvey was deported back to Jamaica, his native country. Isolated from the main body of the organisation, Garvey has been unable to maintain his former autocratic control over the movement, as a result of which there has been a complete disintegration of the organisation, which is now under the control of a number of warring factional leaders. Garvey, who was formerly in the service of American imperialism, has now switched his allegiance to the British, who are utilising him in order to keep the Negro toilers in the British colonies under submission. With this object in view the imperial Government has permitted Garvey to open his headquarters in London.

Despite the bankruptcy of the Garvey movement the ideology of Garveyism, which is the most reactionary expression in Negro bourgeois nationalism, still continues to exert some influence among *certain* sections of the Negro masses. The black landlords and capitalists who support Garveyism are merely trying to mobilise the Negro workers and peasants to support them in establishing a Negro Republic in Africa, where they would be able to set themselves up as the rulers in order to continue the exploitation of the toilers of their race, free from white imperialist competition. In its class content Garveyism is alien to the interests of the Negro toilers. Like *Zionism* and *Gandhism*, it is merely out to utilise racial and national consciousness for the purpose of promoting the class interests of the black bourgeoisie and landlords. In order to further their own aims, the leaders of Garveyism have attempted to utilise the same demagogic methods of appeal used by the leaders of Zionism. For example, they promise to "free" the black workers from all forms of oppression in reward for supporting the utopian programme of "Back to Africa," behind which slogan Garvey attempts to conceal the truly imperialist aims of the Negro bourgeoisie.

The Negro workers must not be deceived by the demagogic gestures of Garvey and his supporters. They must realise that the only way in which they can win their freedom and emancipation is by organising their forces millions strong, and in alliance with the class-conscious white workers in the imperialist countries, as well as the oppressed masses of China, India, Latin America and other colonial and semi-colonial countries, deliver a final blow to world imperialism.

THE END

www.ingramcontent.com/pod-product-compliance
Lightning Source LLC
Chambersburg PA
CBHW021537260326
41914CB00001B/50